MANAGING
TOXIC WASTES

ISSUES FOR THE 90s

MANAGING TOXIC WASTES
by Michael Kronenwetter

THE POOR IN AMERICA
by Suzanne M. Coil

THE WAR ON TERRORISM
by Michael Kronenwetter

ISSUES FOR THE 90s

MANAGING TOXIC WASTES

Michael Kronenwetter

JULIAN MESSNER

JULIAN MESSNER and colophon are trademarks of
Simon & Schuster, Inc. Design by Claire Counihan
Manufactured in the United States of America.

Lib. ed. 10 9 8 7 6 5 4 3 2

Library of Congress Cataloging-in-Publication Data

Kronenwetter, Michael.
Managing toxic wastes.

(Issues for the 90s)
Bibliography: p. 110
Includes index.
Summary: Discusses toxic wastes, their effects on the
environment, their handling and disposal, and government
regulation of such pollutants.
1. Hazardous wastes—United States—Management—
Juvenile literature.   2. Pollution—United States—
Juvenile literature.   [1. Hazardous wastes.   2. Pollu-
tion]   I. Title.   II. Series.
TD1040.K76 1989   363.72'87   89-8236
ISBN 0-671-69051-5 (lib. bdg.)

CONTENTS

MANAGING
TOXIC WASTES

CHAPTER ONE

THE POISONED

ENVIRONMENT

THE United States produces an enormous amount of garbage. From yesterday's newspaper to last year's medicines, from fast-food wrappers carelessly tossed out of car windows to the junked automobiles themselves, we are a wasteful society. We throw away almost as much as we use. Some of what we throw away is dangerous—not just to us, but to generations of people yet to come.

According to the Institute of Chemical Waste Management, about 10 to 15 percent of all the garbage we produce is toxic—that is, it is hazardous either to human health or to the environment. That may sound like a small proportion, but even 10 percent of the enormous amount of garbage we produce adds up to a tremendous amount of hazardous wastes.

The U.S. Environmental Protection Agency, or EPA, estimates that we generate one ton of toxic chemical wastes for every man, woman, and child in the country every year. That only includes what the EPA defines as "solid wastes." (This is a technical definition. The "solid wastes" category includes some liquids and gases when they are stored in certain kinds of containers.) It doesn't include effluents, the wastes that are poured out of factories and sewers into the nation's waterways. Nor does it include what may be the most dangerous of all toxic wastes, the radioactive materials produced by the nuclear power and nuclear weapons industries.

Taken altogether, the EPA estimates that the United States actually spews out about 627 million tons—a staggering 1,254,000,000,000 pounds—of hazardous wastes a year. That's more than two and three-quarters tons for every single person in the country each and every year.

Toxic wastes include many once useful substances, like the chemical fertilizers that help to make American agriculture the most productive in the history of the world, the oil that lubricates our cars and manufacturing machinery, and the chemicals that are essential to the production of most modern conveniences. These things are considered vital to the way we live. It would be hard even to imagine getting along without them.

What happens when their usefulness is over? When the crops have been grown, when the oil has become dirtied and needs to be changed, and when the products have been manufactured? The answer is, all these things ultimately become garbage. They have to be disposed of—abandoned or thrown away or, at the very least, stored to be thrown away later. Unlike other kinds of garbage, however, toxic wastes are not just a problem, they are a threat. Their usefulness may be over, but the danger they present remains.

Carelessly abandoned or inadequately stored toxic wastes can devastate the environment. They can pollute the air and destroy the land and water for great distances around. They can penetrate the topsoil, making it unable to support plant life.

At an empty pharmaceutical plant in Pennsylvania, these barrels of hazardous waste are a potentially poisonous legacy. UPI/Bettmann Newsphotos

They can poison waterways, killing fish, or making them poisonous to people who eat them. They can poison the wells and the groundwater, the underground reserve water that provides much of the water people drink. (Most of the water drunk by rural residents comes from wells that tap into the groundwater. In addition, groundwater provides drinking water for roughly 30 percent of all city residents.) Escaping into the air, toxic wastes can damage the atmosphere itself.

The danger presented by toxic wastes is growing every day—and the danger is worldwide. In the United States we are generating toxic wastes at the rate of 1,718,000 tons a day—but we are not alone. Every country in the world produces its own hazardous wastes. Between us, we are building mountains of solid wastes, rivers of effluents, and a blanket of airborne poisons that threatens to smother us all.

THE MANY FORMS OF TOXIC WASTES

Hazardous wastes come in virtually every form and travel through the environment in almost every way imaginable. They rise into the air as gases and as solids: as fumes from gasoline, and as particulates (bits of matter) in industrial smoke. They are buried in the soil, and they settle onto the land from the air. They pour out into waterways through pipes or seep into them from the groundwater.

The danger represented by toxic wastes can be either short term or long term. Some wastes are only temporarily hazardous. Among these are the wastes that are biodegradable, that is, wastes that can be broken down by such natural processes as the workings of the tiny living creatures known as bacteria. Others are nonbiodegradable. Disposed of in ordinary ways, they will continue to threaten the environment indefinitely. Some are virtually indestructible.

Some problems caused by toxic wastes occur quickly. They are called acute effects and can result from even a brief exposure to the substance. Chronic effects are those that take place over a long period of time. Chronic effects are most often produced by toxic wastes that are carcinogenic, teratogenic, and mutagenic.

Carcinogenic wastes are those capable of causing cancer in human beings or animals.

Teratogenic wastes cause birth defects.

Mutagenic wastes are those that cause harm to the genes of unborn babies. The damaged genes can result in birth defects or diseases, not just to the babies originally exposed to the mutagenic substance, but to their children and to their children's children as well. Many mutagenic substances, including those that are radioactive, are teratogenic as well.

CATEGORIES OF TOXIC WASTES

Wastes can be toxic in many different ways. In general, environmentalists consider a waste toxic if it has any one or more of the following characteristics.

Ignitable wastes catch fire easily. Government agencies define as ignitable anything with a flashpoint under 140 degrees Fahrenheit. A waste is also considered ignitable if it is capable of catching fire through friction. Common ignitable substances include certain paint products, paint thinners, degreasers, and other chemicals called "solvents." (A solvent is any chemical that is used to dissolve other substances.)

Corrosive wastes are those that dissolve metals and other substances or burn the skin. Chemically, they can be either strong acids or bases. They become toxic whenever they are concentrated enough to harm the environment. The Wisconsin Department of Natural Resources, for instance, defines any acid with a pH of 2 or less and any base with a pH of 12.5 or more as corrosive. Such wastes include lye, rust removers, sulphuric acid, hydrochloric acid, battery acid, and some cleaning fluids. They present a particular disposal problem because, over time, they are capable of destroying their containers.

Reactive wastes are those that are chemically unstable. They are called "reactive" because when they combine with some other material, such as water, they react to produce poisonous gases or fumes. Sometimes they even produce explosions. Certain cyanide and sulphur-bearing wastes are included in this category, as are strong oxidizers and bleaches and all explosives.

EP or extraction procedure toxic wastes are those that contain dangerous substances, like pesticides, or heavy metals, like lead, mercury, silver, or cadmium, that could escape into the soil or groundwater. Among the wastes most likely to be EP toxic are grinding dusts, foundary furnace dusts, and wastewater or ink sludges. (A sludge is any kind of slimy or muddy waste deposit.)

Radioactive wastes are those that give off energy, often in the form of gamma rays or invisible charged particles. In large doses, radioactive energy can cause severe burns, illness, or death. Even in much smaller doses it can cause diseases, including cancer and birth defects. Some radioactive substances, such as uranium and radium, occur in nature. Others are generated by industrial processes and in scientific laboratories. Typical radioactive wastes include spent nuclear fuels and parts of old nuclear weapons.

THE NUMBER OF TOXIC WASTES

The sheer numbers of wastes that fit into one or more of the above categories are enormous. Congress listed 698 separate hazardous wastes in the Comprehensive Environmental Response Compensation and Liability Act it passed in 1980. The government's Occupational Safety and Health Administration (OSHA) includes 322 separate items on its list of toxic chemicals alone, while the *Federal Register* lists 402 substances as being not merely hazardous, but "extremely hazardous."

What's more, the number of known toxic wastes is growing all the time. A century ago, very little was known about toxic wastes. Except for acids, bases, and strong poisons, most waste substances were considered safe. Even in 1970, when the EPA began to study the issue, it estimated that the country was generating only 9 million tons of hazardous wastes each year. This drastic underestimation was probably due to the fact that many of the dangerous wastes we know about today had not been studied and were not classified as toxic.

Unfortunately, even today we may be generating many more hazardous wastes than we know about. The National Academy of Science estimates that most of the 60,000 compounds now in use by business and industry still have not been researched for toxicity. There is no way to tell how many of these 60,000 compounds will eventually join the hundreds of others on the lists of toxic substances—or how much harm they are doing in the meantime.

CHAPTER TWO

LOVE CANAL

AND OTHER

HORROR STORIES

MOST of the 250 million tons of solid toxic wastes generated in the United States each year is simply thrown away. Some is buried in the ground in various kinds of dumps and landfills, while some is just dumped on the surface. The EPA has identified more than 25,000 of what it calls "hazardous waste sites" in the United States. There are many more thousands all over the world. These are sites that are so badly contaminated by toxic wastes that they represent a danger to human beings or the environment.

The most unusual toxic waste sites discovered yet were the dead bodies of the beluga whales that recently washed up on the shores of the St. Lawrence Estuary in Canada. The whales had apparently been contaminated by industrial effluents that had been washed into the sea. Their corpses were so saturated with toxic chemicals that the Canadian government officially designated them hazardous waste sites.

Unlike those whales, most hazardous waste sites are places where toxic wastes were deliberately dumped. Some were originally designed for storing wastes and have been carefully maintained in an effort to keep them safe. Others are not. Shockingly, in fact, *most* are not.

Much of the widespread carelessness in storing hazardous wastes has been the result of poor planning or simple sloppiness. Some of the "carelessness," however, has been deliberate. It is the result of greed, a deliberate effort to cut the costs of disposing of the wastes by ignoring safety. When this is done secretly, it is called "midnight dumping." Whether from true carelessness or greed, the EPA estimates that as much as 90 percent of all the wastes produced in the United States each year are unsafely stored.

Regulation of toxic waste disposal varies widely from state to state, but the problem is serious everywhere. Even in a state like Wisconsin, which does a better job than most in handling toxic wastes, only about 24 percent of the hazardous wastes being disposed of each year are buried in landfills that have been licensed to store them safely. Many toxic waste sites across the country have simply been abandoned. No matter how much care was taken when the wastes were first deposited there, no precautions at all are being taken now to protect the environment.

Even more dangerous than the thousands of sites that have been identifed by the EPA are those no one knows about. There's no way to tell how many have been completely forgotten—often built by companies that have long since gone bankrupt. Wastes may be leaching out of these sites even now. There is no way for the people who may be affected by the contamination to protect themselves or even to know that they are in danger.

Of the more than 25,000 "potentially dangerous hazardous

waste sites" the EPA does know about, more than 900 have been put on its national priorities list. These are the sites the EPA believes present "the most serious potential threats to health and the environment." The longer the EPA investigates, though, the longer its national priorities list grows. In the mid-1970s, for example, there were only 638 sites on the list. By the mid-1980s, the list had grown to 888. In 1987, it was expanded again, this time to include 952 serious threats.

For a growing number of people, hazardous waste sites are more than just "serious potential threats." They are personal tragedies. The reality of this fact was first brought home to most Americans in the late 1970s by the terrible events near the Love Canal, in a suburban neighborhood of Niagara Falls, New York.

BEGINNINGS OF A TRAGEDY

The Love Canal started out as a large ditch, dug by a nineteenth-century real estate developer named William Love. He intended to use it to carry water to generate electricity for the prosperous little community he planned to build near the city of Niagara Falls. Love's plans, however, fell through. His community was never built, and Love never turned his ditch into a canal.

Decades later, the abandoned canal was purchased by the Hooker Chemical and Plastics Corporation. For many years after that, the company used the ditch and the land alongside it as a dump for its toxic wastes.

By the early 1950s, the city of Niagara Falls had expanded almost to the banks of the canal. The city wanted the land around the canal to build a school for the children of the young families who were moving into the middle class neighborhood growing up nearby. Under pressure from the city, the chemical company "sold" the canal and the landfill next to it to the school board in 1953 for $1. A new school—known as 99th Street

Elementary—was quickly built on the site. It opened for classes in 1955.

By the 1970s, one generation of children had already grown up in the neighborhood, attending 99th Street school. Most of their families considered the old canal an asset to the community. The children had grown up using the large, open fields bordering it as a playground. Now, many of their own children were doing the same thing.

The parents of this new generation of children were getting frightened. Their children seemed to be getting sick: too sick, too often. Some familiar childhood illnesses, ranging from relatively minor irritations like skin rashes to serious diseases like asthma and kidney disorders, seemed more common in their quiet neighborhood than in other places. There were mysterious illnesses as well. Several children developed unexplained sores on their bodies. Many got painful headaches. Some started bleeding when they went to the toilet. Some became epileptic.

The medical problems started even before the children were born. A study eventually showed that mothers living near Love Canal were more likely than not to have a baby with birth defects. Even more tragically, some babies were never born at all. Miscarriages and stillbirths (babies dead at birth) were becoming more and more frequent.

Something terrible was happening, and the parents of Love Canal children didn't know what it was. It was like a horror story coming true. But this was real life. The parents knew there had to be a reason for the strange and frightening things that were happening to their children. What could it be?

Many parents' suspicions came to center on the area around the canal. There were several mysterious aspects to the area where the children liked to play. Strange substances and objects keep oozing up from the depths of the canal, and some kind of oily sludge occasionally surfaced in the soggy fields nearby. No one seemed to know what that sludge was made of, but puddles

This aerial view of Love Canal dramatically shows the houses and elementary school that lined the area where toxic chemicals were dumped many years before. UPI/Bettmann Newsphotos

of the stuff bubbled up out of the ground from time to time. If a kid fell in, the skin on the exposed parts of his or her body might get red and blister. It could be very painful. It was almost like a burn.

Every now and then, a big metallic drum would heave its rusty back up out of the water. The kids would toss stones at it. It was fun to zing stones off the old cans. It was even fun to miss. When a stone hit the sludge just right, a kind of smoke would rise off the surface of the muck. Sometimes, the sludge itself would make a noise, like some kind of snake monster hissing just below the surface.

Although some parents were suspicious, most told themselves there was nothing serious to worry about. If the canal area were really dangerous, they reasoned, someone would have told them about it. Either the chemical company or the school or the local health authorities would have warned them. There would be a high fence all around the canal to keep the children out. Wouldn't there?

The answer was "no." Some of the chemicals that Hooker Chemical had dumped at Love Canal were very dangerous. Now that they were seeping up into the yards and basements of the neighborhood and into the ground near the school on which the children played, their true nature remained a secret from the people who lived there. No warnings had been given. No fence had been built.

It was only when some residents of the neighborhood grew suspicious enough—and finally outraged enough—to demand explanations that Hooker Chemical and the civic authorities revealed the poisonous secrets of Love Canal.

THE MYSTERY SOLVED

During the many years before the children began to play in the muck over the Love Canal landfill, the company had dumped at least 42 million pounds of various chemicals into the canal. Among them were 13 million pounds of a pesticide called Lindane (benzine hexachloride), known to cause several kinds of cancer, along with several other potentially deadly chemicals. Most deadly of all was the chemical called dioxin, or TCDD. Under the right circumstances, it would only take about three ounces of TCDD to kill everyone in New York City—and several hundred pounds of it had been dumped into Love Canal!

Altogether, later studies identified at least eighty-two different chemical compounds at Love Canal. At least eleven of them were classified as potentially carcinogenic. Many were teratogenic and mutagenic as well.

What's more, the chemicals dumped by Hooker may not have been the only chemicals in the canal. From 1942 to 1945, the city of Niagara Falls had used the site as a garbage dump. Even before that, the U.S. Army may have used the canal to get rid of some of its own toxic wastes.

To be fair, Hooker hadn't simply poured its toxic chemicals into the canal. Most of them had been sealed in metal drums and buried there, some long before the canal had filled up with water. As time went on, some of the containers had become dislodged from their burial place. The drums had worked loose and risen to the surface of the swampy water. Many of the drums—both those in the water and those still underground—eventually developed leaks.

Some of the leaking chemicals spread through the soil; some escaped into the waters of the canal; and some found their way into the groundwater. Traveling in the groundwater, the chemicals made their way under, and finally into, many homes in the neighborhood and into the 99th Street school as well.

Homeowners would suddenly feel their feet slipping into sinkholes of foul, chemical sludge as they mowed their lawns. Other homeowners had no lawns to mow. There were so many poisonous chemicals in the ground that they couldn't make grass grow in their yards.

Men and women were driven out of their own basements by the slimy black sludge that seeped in through cracks in the floors and walls or bubbled up out of the sewer pipes. Families sitting down to Sunday dinner would find their appetites ruined by evil-smelling fumes rising up through the floorboards. The fumes were not just unpleasant to smell. They were dangerous. Tests eventually showed high levels of carcinogenic agents in the air of many homes. Some chemicals were found in concentrations up to 100 times greater than those considered safe by government agencies.

COSTS OF LOVE CANAL

In July 1978, President Jimmy Carter declared Love Canal a federal disaster area. The state of New York quickly relocated more than 250 families away from the Love Canal area. Other nearby families, desperate to leave, were unable to sell their homes because no one wanted to move into the contaminated neighborhood. Finally, the federal government agreed to buy at least 500 of the houses near Love Canal, making $15 million available for the purchase.

A large fence was finally constructed around the canal area to keep children and other potential victims out. Ditches were dug to collect as much of the toxic waste as possible so that it could eventually be removed. Interestingly, the men who dug the ditches were issued gas masks to protect themselves from the same fumes the children had been inhaling for years.

The financial costs of the disaster at Love Canal have been enormous, and they continue to grow. By 1980, the federal government and the state of New York had spent a total of $28 million. In addition, the city of Niagara Falls had spent another $7 million more of its own. The financial costs have continued to mount ever since.

The physical and emotional costs to the people who once lived near the Love Canal have been even greater. All have been badly frightened. Seven hundred families were forced to leave their homes. A test of thirty-six people from the contaminated area showed that eleven of them had suffered chromosome damage. Because it is the chromosomes that transmit hereditary characteristics, any chromosome damage in a parent carries with it a risk to future children.

In addition to the many miscarriages, stillbirths, birth defects, chromosome damage, and physical illnesses that have already occurred, there is fear for the future. There is no way for the former residents of Love Canal to know what the long-term results of their exposure to the toxic chemicals may be.

At the time this book is being written, Love Canal is still badly contaminated. It remains, in the words of one writer, a place "that no one would or could afford to clean." It is a kind of ghost town—a terrible monument to the dangers of toxic wastes.

OTHER TOXIC WASTE HORROR STORIES

News reports from Love Canal shocked the country. The reality of an entire thirty-block neighborhood being poisoned by deadly chemicals both astonished and frightened people. It was particularly ironic that the neighborhood was named "Love," and that it was in the famous vacation city of Niagara Falls: a symbol of natural beauty and the place American newlyweds traditionally visited on their honeymoons.

Somehow, the Love Canal disaster seemed worse than natural disasters like floods or hurricanes. Those are things you couldn't do anything about. Natural disasters strike quickly, do their damage, and are gone. Once they are over, people can pick up the pieces, rebuild, and get on with their lives. Love Canal, however, was a man-made disaster, one whose unpredictable effects would be felt for years to come. What was worse, many people began to wonder if Love Canal was the only tragedy of its kind. Were there other, equally terrible disasters already taking place, undetected, in other neighborhoods throughout the country?

The answer was "yes." There is no way to tell how many, but several other toxic waste disasters have already come to light. Shortly after Love Canal, for example, more than 17,000 metal drums filled with caustic chemicals were discovered in a field near Shepardsville, Kentucky. They were the result of "midnight dumping" that had taken place long before.

Left in an open field, the drums have been exposed to the elements. By the time they were found, many of them had sprung leaks. Many of the caustic chemicals had already seeped into the ground, and some had been washed by the rain into nearby creeks. This so-called Valley of the Drums made clear that Love Canal was not a fluke.

Another notorious example of toxic contamination occurred in rural Missouri. Although the case only came to public

High concentrations of deadly PCB were found in an alley in Detroit, Michigan, in 1986. Here workers hired by the government to clean up the toxic waste fence off a homeowner's property from the contaminated alley. UPI/Bettmann Newsphotos

attention in the early 1980s, the contamination had begun in the 1970s, when oil that had been carelessly mixed with dioxin had been sprayed onto dirt roads to keep down the dust. In the process, the TCDD contaminated not only the roads themselves, but the surrounding soil and water as well.

Spread by wind and rain, the dioxin-contaminated dust had worked its way into the nearby small town of Times Beach, Missouri. There, it got into everything, even the tiniest crevices of the town's wooden buildings. Tests in 1982 showed that dioxin levels in the town were more than 100 times higher than was considered safe.

The EPA ordered the town evacuated while it removed the dioxin. That proved impossible to do, however. The town was so thoroughly contaminated that there was no way to clean it up. Finally, in 1983, the government offered to purchase the entire town of Times Beach for $33 million.

Highly publicized areas like Love Canal and Times Beach are only tips of a huge iceberg, or, rather, they are peaks of an enormous mountain of poisonous trash that is rising up over our country at the rate of more than 1.4 billion pounds a day. Less publicized cases are occurring all the time.

It hardly made a ripple in the national press when eight Lowell, Massachusetts, families were forced to leave their homes in the spring of 1988. "Blue dirt" containing a cyanide had begun to rise out of the ground into the driveways and yards of their expensive homes. The cyanide apparently had been buried under the lots before the homes were built on them.

The families living there believed the contaminated dirt was responsible for asthma and miscarriages they had suffered. The state of Massachusetts claimed the poison-containing dirt presented little actual danger to the families' health, but its actions belied its claims. Much as New York had done in the case of Love Canal, the state of Massachusetts paid to move the families out of the contaminated neighborhood. Unlike New York, however, Massachusetts claimed that the move was only temporary. The families would be housed elsewhere only for a year or so, the time it would take to test the neighborhood thoroughly. The families, however, were far from satisfied. They demanded more than just testing. They wanted a complete cleanup of the toxic dirt buried under their homes before they would return.

Now that we have seen some of what toxic wastes in the ground and waterways can do, it is time to examine just what they are and where they come from.

CHAPTER THREE

THREATS TO

LAND AND WATER

SOLID toxic wastes began piling up in what is now the United States as early as the 1750s, when the first coal mine was dug in Virginia. When rain washes through the wastes from a coal mining operation, the water becomes contaminated with acid. When this acidic water runs off into nearby waterways, it can kill fish and poison human water supplies.

The production of toxic wastes was speeded up by the Industrial Revolution. The new machines of the late eighteenth and nineteenth centuries spewed out toxic wastes at a rate that couldn't even have been imagined a century earlier. Then, in 1859, the discovery of oil in Titusville, Pennsylvania, led to the development of whole new forms of toxic wastes, and the rapidly developing chemical and nuclear industries of the twentieth century have led to hundreds more.

There is not enough space in this book to discuss or even to name all of the many hundreds of solid and liquid toxic wastes. The following, however, are some of the most common—and the most dangerous.

ASBESTOS

Asbestos is the general name for a large category of mineral fibers. The fibers share several characteristics that once made them popular for use in a variety of products. Being resistant to both heat and electricity, for example, asbestos has been widely used as insulation for buildings, furnaces, heat-carrying pipes, and even electrical wires. Because it can be woven into cloth, it has been used to make fireproof clothing and other products. In addition, it was widely used in construction materials, including some plasters and plasterboards, and as a key ingredient in automobile, truck, and bus brakes.

Once considered a "miracle material," it is only recently that scientists have discovered how dangerous asbestos really is. Materials that contain asbestos tend to break down over time, and they release asbestos fibers into the air. Often, the fibers are so small that they can't even be seen with the naked eye.

Whether inhaled from the air or ingested in food or water, the fibers can settle in the lungs or travel through the blood stream and lodge in other parts of the body. Once there, they irritate the body's living cells. Because the fibers are all but indestructible, the irritation can go on for years, even decades. This constant irritation can provoke cancerous responses from the body, including a particularly deadly form of the disease called "asbestosis."

The use of asbestos has been sharply cut back in recent years. The EPA called for a ban on most uses of asbestos in 1986, and it hopes for complete elimination of asbestos use within ten years. In the meantime, however, hundreds of asbestos products remain in the environment, waiting to release their deadly fibers. It is dangerous even to attempt to remove a product that

In the past, asbestos was often used as insulation in schools and other buildings across the United States. The discovery of asbestos in the ceiling of this New York City school caused parents to pressure authorities to close the school. UPI/Bettmann Newsphotos

contains asbestos because of the likelihood that fibers will be released. In recent years, a whole industry has sprung up that specializes in removing asbestos-containing products from schools, homes, and other buildings.

HEAVY METALS

We don't usually think of metals as foods. Some metals can, in fact, be important elements of the human diet. They can be either nutrients or poisons. Some are both. Zinc, for example, is

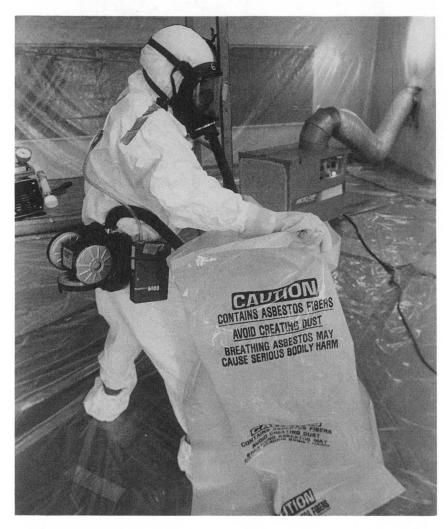

Asbestos fibers are so dangerous that workers who remove the material from buildings must wear special protective clothing and seal off the cleanup area with sheets of plastic. UPI/Bettmann Newsphotos

vital to human growth and is an important element of insulin. In large amounts, however, it can be a deadly poison.

Zinc and Cadmium
Zinc and cadmium are very similar to each other. Both are used to coat other metals to protect them against corrosion, and both

are commonly contained in electrical batteries, tires, and other rubber products. Additionally, each has important uses of its own. Cadmium, for example, is an important ingredient in fireworks, while zinc is the substance that lights up television screens. Both are equally dangerous. They are members of a group of toxic elements known as "heavy" metals, which includes familiar metals like lead and mercury, as well as such exotic metals as beryllium.

Lead

Lead is widely used in paints, coatings that protect metal surfaces from rust, matches, and electric batteries. For decades, it was also used as an ingredient in most gasolines because it helps keep car engines from knocking.

Like several other metals, lead is fat soluble, which means that it can be dissolved and stored in fats. When small amounts of lead are ingested into the body, the body stores them in its fat cells. As more and more amounts of lead are ingested, they accumulate in higher and higher concentrations within the body's fat cells, until enough has been collected to make a person sick. We now know that long-term exposure to lead interferes with the workings of the intestines, heart, kidneys, brain, and central nervous system. When enough lead accumulates, it can even kill.

Historically, lead poisoning has been most common among workers exposed to lead on their jobs, like painters who regularly inhale the fumes of lead-based paints. The general public is also exposed to lead: particularly the lead in the air that comes from gasoline fumes. Tragically, many children have been poisoned by chewing on bits of leaded paint that peel off the walls and furniture in old houses.

Mercury

Mercury is extremely useful. It is a key element in a variety of products, ranging from thermometers to oil paints, and from insecticides to dental fillings. When it gets inside the human body, though, mercury attacks the tissues. It can cause blindness, deafness, and hemorrhages, as well as damage to the intestines, liver, kidneys, brain, and nervous system. The well-known phrase "mad as a hatter" comes from the fact that many nineteenth-century hat makers developed nervous disorders from being poisoned by the mercury they used in processing beaver hides to make felt.

Mercury used in manufacturing and agricultural processes is sometimes discharged into waterways, where it enters the human food chain. Many people around the world have been poisoned by eating fish contaminated with mercury.

In the small quantities likely to be found in one or two poisoned fish, mercury is relatively harmless. Like lead, however, mercury can build up in the body. If too many mercury-contaminated fish are eaten, serious health problems can result. Just how serious those problems can be was tragically demonstrated at Minamata Bay, Japan. For centuries, the people who lived around the bay relied on fish and other seafood for the bulk of their diet. In the 1950s, a local chemical company began dumping mercuric chloride, a compound of mercury and chlorine, into the bay. Without anyone realizing it, the fish were contaminated by the mercury.

Before long, many people who lived near the bay began to have mysterious symptoms. Their hands and feet would feel strange to them. They began to shake and tremble for no apparent reason. They were unable to talk clearly. Soon, animals around the bay began to die, thrashing wildly on the ground. Eventually, people began to die, too—many of them also writhing in intense agony. The strange illnesses at Minamata Bay continued until the early 1970s before they were diagnosed as mercury poisoning. By that time, more than 3,500 people had been poisoned.

Beryllium
Exotic beryllium is a true space age metal. Because other metals become both lighter and stronger when alloyed (or combined)

with beryllium, it is used in parts of aircraft and rockets. It is also a key ingredient in some solid rocket fuels and is widely used in the electronics and nuclear power industries. Beryllium compounds help to increase the carrying capacity of communication systems, and the metal is used to form a protective "blanket" over the cores of nuclear reactors.

In the forms in which beryllium is finally used, it is not particularly dangerous. When beryllium is used in the manufacturing process, however, dust and fumes containing bits of the metal are given off. Even a tiny amount of this beryllium dust can be deadly if inhaled into the human body.

Disposal

Among the many other toxic metals are silver, copper, nickel, and selenium. Like some of those discussed above, most are carcinogenic. They also share another characteristic, one that makes them especially difficult to dispose of safely: their persistence.

Unlike some other toxic substances, heavy metals are not destroyed by the ordinary workings of time and nature. They don't break down into separate, less dangerous elements. They are elements themselves. No matter how they are disposed of, they remain stubbornly toxic indefinitely.

Burying toxic metals, in whatever form, presents the constant danger that they will leach into the ground, meaning that rain or some other force will carry bits of them into the surrounding soil or groundwater. A hard rain, for example, can wash cadmium from an old battery into a nearby stream or river.

Although the metals themselves cannot be broken down, compounds containing metals can. Metals are often found in compounds. Oxides, for example, are combinations of metals and oxygen. Sulfides are combinations of metals and sulphur. Because of the tendency of many metal compounds to break down, metals that were once held fast in apparently harmless chemical compounds can leach into the soil or water. An apparently "safe" beryllium compound can break up over time, and the beryllium can seep into the soil. Because of their persistence, toxic metals will remain a threat to leach into the environment for centuries after they are buried.

ARSENIC

Arsenic is a transition element, which means that it sometimes behaves like a metal, and sometimes it does not. This versatility is one of its major assets. Arsenic is used in a large variety of goods, from ordinary glass to the most sophisticated semiconductors. It is an important alloy, helping to make metals stronger, harder, and more resistant to corrosion. Because it acts to preserve skins and leathers, it is used in both tanning and taxidermy.

Even arsenic's high toxicity has been put to use. It is not only used in many animal poisons and insecticides, it is a key ingredient in admasite and lewisite—two of the most deadly gases ever developed for chemical warfare.

People exposed to even low levels of arsenic over long periods of time tend to become sickly and gradually "waste away." Those exposed to a large dose can die at once. Whether taken all at once or over a long period of time, however, one grain of arsenic is enough to kill.

Although arsenic has been regulated by the EPA ever since the late 1970s, cases of arsenic contamination continue to occur. Ten of the 350 hazardous waste sites examined by the EPA in 1980 were found to contain raw arsenic.

TOXIC HYDROCARBONS

Most of the 322 chemicals on OSHA's list of hazardous chemicals are compounds: combinations of different elements, at least some of which are not harmful by themselves. One of the largest and most dangerous groups of toxic compounds is the hydrocarbons. Hydrocarbons are the compounds of hydrogen and carbon. Usually derived from petroleum or coal tar, they are often manufactured for use in industry.

Benzene is one of the most toxic of all hydrocarbons. A colorless, pleasant-smelling liquid, it is used in making drugs, dyes, synthetic rubber, and plastics, among many other products. It is both flammable and highly carcinogenic and known to be a significant cause of leukemia and aplastic anemia. In the EPA's 1980 study of 350 hazardous waste sites in the United States, benzene and similar compounds were found at more sites (132) than any other major class of chemicals except the chlorines. Additionally, benzene is a major air pollutant.

Halogenated hydrocarbons are produced when hydrocarbons are combined with chlorine, bromine, or iodine. Trichlorophenol, or TCP, for example, is a combination of a hydrocarbon known as a phenol with chlorine. A corrosive poison, TCP is used in the manufacture of herbicides, or weed killers. Carelessly mixed with waste oil, however, TCP has shown up in several cases of contamination resulting from spraying oil on dirt roads.

Overheating TCP in the manufacturing process results in an even deadlier chemical—tetrachlorodibenzo-para-dioxin—which we have already met as TCDD, or dioxin. A major villain in both Love Canal and Times Beach, dioxin may be the single most powerful cancer-causing agent known. Besides being carcinogenic, dioxin is teratogenic and probably mutagenic as well. Some environmentalists consider it the most deadly of all chemicals because it can produce fatal effects with extremely low concentrations.

Another group of halogenated hydrocarbons, the polychlorinated biphenyls, or PCBs, has the distinction of being the only class of chemicals whose manufacture has been totally banned by an act of the U.S. Congress. Like mercury, PCBs tend to invade the human diet through fish that have been contaminated by eating algae and other small creatures that have been poisoned by PCBs in the water.

PCBs get into waterways in two main ways: first, in effluents discharged by manufacturing companies and, second, as the result of incineration. For many years, PCBs were commonly used in the manufacture of electrical equipment and as an ingredient in some kinds of plastics, papers, insulating liquids, and hydraulic fluids. When these products eventually outlive their usefulness and are incinerated, the PCBs are released into the air. Either by sticking to falling dust particles or dropping with the rain, some of these PCBs fall into rivers, lakes, and streams. There, they are collected in the tiny organisms eaten by fish. As the small fish eat the contaminated microorganisms, the PCBs are stored in their bodies. When larger fish eat them, the concentrated PCBs become even more concentrated in *their* cells. This process, called "bioconcentration," means that some fish can have very high concentrations of chemicals in their bodies, even when the concentration levels in the water itself are low. This, of course, can make those fish dangerous to eat.

PCBs are carcinogenic. In addition, they are suspected of causing a variety of other ailments, including hair loss, serious reproductive problems, and liver disease. Even though PCBs are no longer manufactured in the United States, electrical transformers and other products containing them are still in use. They will all eventually become waste and have to be disposed of. Making the problem worse is the fact that PCBs seem to be nearly as persistent as the heavy metals. Under most conditions, PCBs can remain hazardous for centuries.

Polybrominated biphenyl, or PBB, is a flame-retardant relative of the PCBs. It, too, is extremely persistent. Once it gets into the food chain it is likely to stay there for a long time. Hundreds of pounds of powdered PBB were inadvertantly mixed with cattle feed in Michigan in 1974. Before the mistake was discovered, the feed had been used on hundreds of dairy farms throughout the state. Many thousands of cows were poisoned. Because the powder in the cattle feed had been scattered around farm yards by the wind, many chickens and sheep were infected, too.

Altogether, thousands of sheep, tens of thousands of dairy cattle, and millions of chickens either died from the chemicals or had to be killed to protect the food supply. And, in spite of attempts to clean up the PBB contamination in 1974, the poisonous powder continued to show up on some Michigan farms—and in some farm animals—years later.

Because PBBs can be passed along the food chain, people who ate the dairy products, meats, and eggs from the poisoned animals were exposed to PBBs themselves. There is no way to tell just how many people actually ate the contaminated food. It has been estimated, however, that most of the population of Michigan was probably exposed to the PBBs.

Those who received the heaviest doses of the chemical were probably the members of the farm families who used the contaminated feed for their own animals. Many of them complained of stomachaches, hair loss, tiredness, headaches, and dizziness. Some believed that their memories had been affected as well.

Unfortunately, there has not been enough scientific research on PBBs to understand what the long-term medical effects of this widespread exposure to the chemical are likely to be. The same is true of many other substances discussed in this chapter and of most other toxic wastes as well. We know that they are dangerous and that significant exposure to them may result in harmful effects years—and even decades—later. But the extent of the danger is unknown.

NUCLEAR WASTES

For many people, the radioactive wastes generated by the nucler power and nuclear weapons industries are the most frightening of all toxic wastes.

Nuclear power is produced by two processes: fission and fusion. Although these processes are, in a sense, opposites, each involves a change in the nuclei (or centers) of atoms. Those changes release energy that was previously held in check inside the atoms themselves.

In fission, the nuclei of special atoms (usually of a kind of uranium known as U-235) are split in two. The pieces of the first atoms to be smashed fly outward, slamming into the nuclei of nearby atoms and smashing them in turn. The result is a chain reaction involving millions and millions of the tiny atoms, which releases an enormous amount of energy.

In fusion, the nuclei of neighboring atoms are not smashed but joined—or fused—together under intense heat. Their fusion forms atoms of a different kind altogether. When the new atoms are lighter than the combined weights of the original atoms, the extra weight is given off as energy. The fuels used for fusion are particularly heavy forms of hydrogen atoms, which join to form much lighter helium atoms.

Because fusion releases much more energy than fission, fusion is used in the most powerful of weapons, thermonuclear bombs. The heat for the fusion reaction in such weapons is provided by a fission explosion. The nuclear power industry, which requires the release of smaller amounts of energy over a longer time, uses only the more controllable fission process.

Both forms of nuclear energy production leave large amounts of radioactive wastes behind. Nuclear fission, for example, uses up only about two-thirds of the radioactive energy in fuel rods of U-235. The third left over remains a potentially devastating threat to human health and the environment. Even an unexploded thermonuclear weapon contains substantial amounts of extremely radioactive heavy hydrogen in liquid form.

These wastes present special disposal problems. Like toxic metals, they are incredibly persistent. Although they become less radioactive over time, that process takes thousands upon thousands of years. Additionally, radioactive wastes can make other substances radioactive as well. Even the pools of water used to cool down nuclear fuel rods in nuclear power plants become radioactive.

There are two major categories of radioactive wastes: high level and low level. Both are dangerous. Even a brief exposure to the intense radiation given off by high-level wastes can kill: sometimes immediately and sometimes through the slower process of radiation sickness. Low-level wastes are not as intensely toxic, but they can still be deadly. Longer exposure to them can produce cancers and other deadly diseases.

A sign of just how dangerous nuclear materials can be was demonstrated by the aftermath of an accident at a nuclear power plant at Chernobyl, in the Soviet Union, in April 1986. A fire in the plant's nuclear reactor sent a cloud of deadly radiation into the air that was strong enough to be detected around the world. Information on the immediate effects of the accident was unreliable, but it was clear that some people in the plant died right away, and scores of people in the vicinity quickly came down with radiation sickness. Many died soon after. More important, medical experts predicted that as many as 24,000 people were likely to die in the future from illnesses caused by the escaped radiation.

The accident at Chernobyl involved an active nuclear reactor. Another disaster, however, could release radiation from stored high-level nuclear wastes as well. The aftermath of Chernobyl clearly demonstrates the dangers of a major escape of nuclear radiation, whatever its source.

Here in the United States, there have been several less serious cases of nuclear accidents. Some, like the famous one at Three Mile Island in Pennsylvania, involved civilian power plants. Others involved the storage of military wastes. In 1973, for example, 115,000 gallons of liquid nuclear wastes leaked from a military storage tank in Hanford, Washington.

As early as 1980, at least 2,700 metric tons (5,952,420 pounds) of radioactive wastes from nuclear power plants and at least 60 million gallons of radioactive wastes from the nuclear weapons industry, were being stored in the United States. More and more nuclear wastes have been piling up ever since. Incredibly, these wastes can be stored only in temporary sites. No way has yet been found to store them safely for the 10,000 years or more they will remain dangerous. (What plans there are will be discussed in Chapter 6.)

CHAPTER FOUR

TOXIC WASTES

IN THE AIR

WHEN most people hear the term *toxic wastes*, they think of substances that people have disposed of in very deliberate ways. They picture steel drums filled with chemicals, streams of effluents pouring out of factory pipes. However, not all the toxic wastes of modern society are buried or poured out into waterways.

There are other kinds of toxic wastes, including gases and tiny droplets of liquids, as well as ash and other solid particles that can travel in fumes or smoke. Most of them are by-products of industrial processes or of the combustion of fuels. They are, in a sense, unintentional and almost neglected wastes. It has been easy to neglect them. Unlike more bulky wastes, little effort has been made to dispose of them. They can be allowed simply to escape into the air. They are, however, at least as dangerous to health and the environment as the more obviously troublesome solid and liquid wastes dealt with in the previous chapters.

The damage done by toxic chemicals in the soil and water is limited by where and how far they can travel. Airborne wastes, though, are not limited by geography or geology. They can threaten not just specific places and specific groups of people, they can threaten the very structure of the atmosphere itself: the life system of the whole planet.

CARBON MONOXIDE

Many airborne wastes are by-products of burning fossil fuels. Fossil fuels are those that have been formed, over time, from decayed animal and vegetable matter. They include petroleum-based fuels like gasoline, as well as coal and natural gas. Fossil fuels are rarely if ever completely consumed by burning. Instead, the inefficient burning process gives off carbon as waste. The carbon is often released into the air in molecules of compounds made up of carbon atoms and oxygen atoms: either as carbon monoxide (CO) or carbon dioxide (CO_2).

Carbon monoxide is a deadly gas that can't be seen, smelled, or tasted. It is given off in several ways, one of which is as one of the most dangerous toxic components of tobacco smoke. Most of the carbon monoxide that gets into the air, however, is the product of inefficient burning of gasoline in car engines.

When inhaled, carbon monoxide interferes with the body's use of oxygen. When we breathe, oxygen is taken into our lungs and absorbed into our blood. The blood carries the oxygen to all the cells of our bodies, which need oxygen in order to live. Carbon monoxide is absorbed into the blood even more easily than oxygen. So, when a person breathes air containing carbon monoxide, the carbon monoxide tends to take the place of oxygen in the person's blood. As a result, the body's cells are starved of oxygen, and the body can die.

The effects of carbon monoxide in the air are usually not

noticeable in well-ventilated areas. However, carbon monoxide can build up to dangerous levels in heavy traffic or in parking lots and garages. People who spend a lot of time in such conditions may become unnaturally tired. Their vision may be blurred, and their physical responses and mental judgments may be affected. People already suffering from heart conditions that affect the supply of oxygen in their blood can be put in serious danger.

The drowsiness produced by carbon monoxide can threaten even healthy drivers of cars with ineffective exhaust systems. If carbon monoxide leaks into the passenger compartment of a poorly ventilated car, the chemical can build up to dangerous, even fatal, levels inside the car.

OZONE

Ozone is an unusual air pollutant in that it is made up entirely of oxygen. Each molecule of ozone (or O_3) is made up of three atoms of oxygen. Although ordinary oxygen is the main element of the air we breathe, ozone is a menace. It is, in fact, the main element in the kind of air pollution called "smog."

Ozone irritates mucous membranes and lung tissues. Some scientists believe that it even makes the lungs more vulnerable to infections. Because it damages the body's ability to breathe— that is, to use oxygen efficiently—it presents a particular danger to people with respiratory diseases or heart problems.

In addition, ozone is a threat both to the natural environment and to many man-made products. It interferes with the process of photosynthesis by which green plants convert carbon dioxide into energy. It also attacks certain synthetic fabrics, as well as rubber products.

Ozone is not a toxic waste, but is formed in the air from other substances that are, including nitrogen oxides (compounds made up of nitrogen and oxygen) and volatile organic compounds (VOCs). VOCs are fumes given off by gasoline, paints,

Weather conditions can trap ozone and other pollutants in a low-lying cloud, as seen in this photograph of the Denver, Colorado, skyline. UPI/Bettmann Newsphotos

degreasing agents, and various cleaning fluids. If you've ever noticed shimmering in the air over a car's open gas tank, you've seen volatile organic compounds escaping into the atmosphere.

Like carbon monoxide, nitrogen oxides are given off in the exhausts of automobiles. They are also given off, along with several other air pollutants, in industrial smoke. When these oxides meet VOCs in the air in the presence of sunshine, the result is the chemical reaction by which ozone is formed.

Because both VOCs and nitrogen oxides are associated with automobiles, ozone pollution tends to be heaviest in the air over big cities. Because ozone formation is encouraged by sunshine, sunny cities like Los Angeles and Denver tend to have the biggest problems with it.

Most of the harm done to people by ozone and other kinds of smog can be either acute but relatively minor or chronic and more serious. An example of acute harm might be momentary shortness of breath. A chronic effect might be a serious lung disease. Certain weather conditions can trap large quantities of ozone, sulphur dioxide, and other industrial air pollutants within a specific geographical area. At such times, the effects of the smog can be not only acute, but deadly. Because such events often take place over heavily crowded urban areas, the threat to life can be extreme.

London, England, has long been infamous for its killer fogs. One thousand people died there in one of the first such incidents in 1880; and 4,000 people died in London in 1952, in the single worst killer fog disaster in history. Killer fogs are not limited to London, though. Hundreds of people have died in incidents in New York City, 168 of them as recently as 1966.

NITROGEN AND SULPHUR OXIDES AND ACID RAIN

The same nitrogen oxide that takes part in the formation of ozone can be dangerous in other ways. Falling rain washes tiny particles of nitrogen oxides, as well as sulphur oxides, from the air. Nitrogen and sulphur atoms from these compounds can combine with hydrogen atoms in the rain to form sulphuric and nitric acids. These acids then fall to earth with the rain. This so-called acid rain has become a serious threat to the environment of large areas of the world, including the northeastern United States and Canada.

"Throughout North America," warns Canada's Environment Minister Tom McMillan, "the single most serious environmental threat is acid rain. [It] destroys thousands of lakes and rivers, kills whole fish populations, undermines tourism and agriculture, retards forest growth, erodes the built heritage, and threatens human health."

North America is not the only part of the world that suffers from acid rain. In Norway and Sweden, some lakes and rivers have lost whole varieties of fish to acid rain, while 34 percent of the forests of West Germany have been damaged by it. There is real fear that Germany's fabled Black Forest may be destroyed.

While there is some controversy over the source of acid rain, most scientists believe that the main sources of the problem are automobiles, which emit nitrogen oxides into the air, and industrial plants, which emit both nitrogen and sulphur oxides. Whatever their source, airborne oxides can travel for hundreds of miles before being washed down to earth with the rain. This means that, although the places that suffer most from acid rain tend to be forest regions and waterways, the true source of the problem is in the big cities and industrial areas.

CARBON DIOXIDE AND THE GREENHOUSE EFFECT

Like its close relative carbon monoxide, carbon dioxide (CO_2) is a colorless, odorless, and tasteless gas. It is released into the atmosphere in several ways: by human breathing, by fermentation of sugars, and by the burning of fossil fuels. By far the biggest generator of carbon dioxide is the automobile, which releases it as a by-product of burning gasoline. It has been estimated, for example, that a single automobile in a major city gives off more carbon dioxide than the breathing of all the people who live there.

Unlike carbon monoxide, carbon dioxide has many innocent uses. It is the substance that causes bread dough to rise. It is what puts the fizziness in soft drinks. It is the fuel green plants use for photosynthesis. When released into the air, however, carbon dioxide can be even more dangerous than carbon monoxide. It is, however, dangerous in a very different way. Instead of endangering the health of individual people and animals, it threatens the environment as a whole. According to most experts, the buildup of carbon dioxide in the atmosphere is beginning to affect the climate of the entire world.

As Canada's Environment Minister Tom McMillan said,

A German forestry official points out the effect of acid rain on fir trees near Bonn, West Germany. AP/Wide World Photos

carbon dioxide from burning fossil fuels and certain less important pollutants "are accumulating in the atmosphere and trapping solar energy reflected from earth. The result is an increase in surface temperature—the so-called 'greenhouse effect.'" It is called this because the canopy of pollutants acts like the roof and sides of a greenhouse. They let the sun's heat energy in and then trap it there, causing the temperature inside to rise. The result, if this takes place over the whole Earth, could be disastrous. McMillan warns that "scientists predict an average global warming of about four degrees centigrade within the next 45 years."

Four degrees may not sound like very much. In most places, the temperature rises and falls by much more than that almost every day. When applied to the world's climate as a whole, however, four degrees is an enormous increase. According to David Rind, a climate researcher for the National Aeronautics and Space Administration, four degrees is as much as the temperature of the world has risen in the entire 11,000 years since the end of the last Ice Age.

What effects would that kind of rise in temperature have in the future? According to McMillan, "A global change of four degrees within such a short time will alter precipitation patterns and vegetation zones throughout the world, with potentially disastrous consequences in some regions."

Most climatologists agree that the buildup of carbon dioxide is already in the process of generating a "greenhouse effect." Some are convinced that the "potentially disastrous consequences" have already begun. They point out, for example, that the four hottest years on record have all occurred in the 1980s.

CHLOROFLUOROCARBONS, HALONS, AND THE THREAT TO THE OZONE LAYER

Although ozone is a threat to human health when it is found close to the ground, high up in the stratosphere it is a protector. Thirty miles and more above the earth, a layer of ozone acts as a kind of shield, protecting the earth from the worst of the sun's deadly ultraviolet radiation.

The ozone that makes up this protective layer is formed by the action of that same ultraviolet radiation on oxygen in the atmosphere. In the process of absorbing the radiation, some oxygen atoms combine to form molecules of ozone. The ozone then absorbs even more of the ultraviolet radiation, which stops it from traveling to earth.

Many scientists believe that the vital ozone shield is being threatened by a number of chemical compounds, including nitrogen oxides. It is ironic that nitrogen oxides, which combine with VOCs in the lower atmosphere to *form* ozone, tend to *break down* ozone in the stratosphere. The nitrogen oxides found high above the earth seem to be mostly those released by nitrogen fertilizers used in agriculture and in the exhausts of some jet aircraft.

The main threat to the ozone layer doesn't come from nitrogen oxides, however, but from chlorofluorocarbons and halons. Chlorofluorocarbons (CFCs) are synthetically produced compounds, made up of atoms of chlorine, fluorine, and carbon. In addition to their disastrous effect on the ozone layer, chlorofluorocarbons contribute about 20 percent of the chemicals that produce the greenhouse effect. Halons are similar to chlorofluorocarbons, but include bromine atoms as well. Sometimes called freons, these compounds are used in air-conditioning and refrigeration products, as well as in spray cans and fire extinguishers. Others are used by the electronics industry as cleaning agents and by the chemical industry in the manufacture of foam products.

Scientists, including many working for governments all around the world, believe that these compounds are destroying the protective ozone layer. Although chlorofluorocarbons and halons seem to be safe in the forms in which they were originally used on earth, they can escape into the air and rise into the upper atmosphere. There, the sun's ultraviolet rays break down the originally "safe" compounds, releasing the chlorine and bromine atoms trapped inside.

Just a single atom of chlorine can destroy 10,000 atoms of ozone, while a single atom of bromine can destroy 100,000 ozone atoms. At current rates, nearly 1 million tons of the destructive chlorofluorocarbons and halons are being released into the atmosphere every year. The result is a potential disaster.

There is some evidence that the disaster is already beginning. For years, scientists have reported evidence of a hole in the ozone layer over the Earth's poles. In August 1988, for the first time, the Soviet Union reported measuring a thinning of the ozone layer over some of its largest cities. Although the thinning proved temporary, scientists were alarmed. This was the most dramatic sign yet that the ozone layer may be breaking down over heavily populated areas.

According to *Environment Update* magazine: "A depletion of ozone would lead to increased skin cancer and eye disease, such as cataracts, and could adversely affect the body's immune system." These direct physical effects would not be the worst of the damage. "Ozone depletion would seriously affect the world's ability to feed itself. Increased ultraviolet light would reduce crop yields worldwide and damage small organisms at the base of [the] aquatic food chain, affecting fisheries." In addition, ozone depletion would add to the intensity of the greenhouse effect.

"If the release of the offending gases is not curtailed sharply," warns Tom McMillan, "the ozone shield may effectively disappear by the year 2040." The destruction of that shield is already under way. What's more, the ozone-eating chemicals remain active for so long, according to *Environment Update,* that even if the industries of the world stop releasing them today, "the depletion of the ozone layer [would] continue for at least a hundred years."

IMMEDIATE THREATS

Scientists have been warning governments of the dangers of airborne toxic wastes for many decades. Governments have been slow, though, to act on their warnings. The dangers of acid rain, for example, have become steadily clearer throughout the 1980s, and yet the U.S. government has continued to insist that more study is needed before action can be taken to combat the problem. The government was so slow to act, in fact, that Congressman David Obey complained that it "has dragged its feet through more than 6,000 studies on acid rain while we have watched forests and lakes die."

As we will see in future chapters, it is only relatively recently that the U.S. government has begun to move strongly against the threat of any kind of toxic waste. Some people are already worried that it may be too late. As former President Jimmy Carter warned at the 1988 National Democratic Convention, "The greenhouse effect, the destruction of the ozone layer, and acid rain are no longer just theoretical possibilities. They are immediate threats to all of us."

CHAPTER FIVE

WHO IS TO BLAME?

THE mountain of toxic waste that looms over the United States was not heaved up out of the earth by volcanic forces. Nor was it the product of some Natural disaster like a hurricane, flood, or tornado. It is a man-made mountain of materials that threaten our lives.

Who are the people who built this mountain? What kind of people must they be? Who could be so careless as to risk damaging the environment that supports us and even the ozone layer that protects us? Who would dare to risk changing the climate of the entire Earth in possibly disastrous ways? Who could be so heartless that they would risk poisoning us all—and future generations as well?

Who is really to blame for all these toxic wastes? There are many, many answers to that question.

MINING

In many ways, toxic waste began with mining. Coal mining was the first industry to generate toxic wastes in what is now the United States. For that reason, the toxic waste problem on this continent can be dated to the 1750s, when the first coal mine was dug in Virginia. Today, mining is the main direct source of most of the substances that eventually get discarded as toxic wastes. These include not only fossil fuels, but heavy metals and radioactive materials as well. In the process of pulling them out of the Earth, the mining industry builds many toxic mountains of its own.

The amount of wastes produced by the mining industry is staggering. The EPA estimates that mining of all kinds produces more than 2 billion tons of solid wastes in the United States each year. The production of a single ton of copper, for instance, generates more than 500 tons of solid wastes, along with many more tons of air pollutants. Although only a small proportion of those solid wastes are toxic, it is more than enough to threaten nearby water supplies. A 1980 study revealed that about one-third of all the waters leaching from U.S. copper mine wastes were contaminated.

Of the forms of mining that produce hazards to the environment, coal mining is considered to be the greatest threat. Hills of coal mining wastes, known as slag, stud the countryside in the coal mining regions of Appalachia. These black piles often start smouldering of their own accord, burning on like huge charcoal grills, and sending dirty, foul-smelling smoke into the air. Thousands of miles of American waterways have been contaminated by sulphuric acid that originated in coal mining wastes. When rain filters through these sulphur rich wastes, the sulphuric acid that is formed drains into the groundwater or runs off into nearby rivers and streams, killing fish and spoiling the water supply.

Sulphuric acid is not the only harmful substance that is drained from mine tailings. (*Tailings* is the general term for the many forms of solid wastes that result from mining processes.) Lead, zinc, and cyanide are among the many other toxic substances that are often found in drainage from mining wastes.

MANUFACTURING INDUSTRIES

When the EPA conducted a survey of the major generators of hazardous wastes in 1981, it found that 85 percent of them were involved in manufacturing. Almost all manufacturing industries use solvents to clean their machinery. In addition, most generate various kinds of reactive and ignitable wastes. Manufacturers of metal products generate large quantities of acids and bases and often produce wastes contaminated with heavy metals as well. The textile, plastics, leather, and paint industries are also significant producers of wastes containing heavy metals. Pulp and paper mills generate large amounts of chemical wastes, including benzene, and the pharmaceutical (or drug) industry is the leading producer of arsenic-contaminated wastes.

By far the biggest industrial generators of solid toxic wastes are the chemical and petroleum industries. These include the petrochemical companies that specialize in making chemicals out of petroleum. The great majority of the United States' most dangerous hazardous waste sites, as determined by the EPA, were generated by the chemical, petroleum, or petrochemical industries. (Among them, of course, was Love Canal.)

Industrial plants of all kinds are also major generators of airborne hazardous wastes. Along with the usual by-products of fossil fuel combustion, common industrial air pollutants include arsenic, antimony, barium, chlorine, cyanide, lead, nickel, and mercury compounds, as well as the alkaline particles known as fly ash.

OTHER BUSINESSES, LARGE AND SMALL

Manufacturing industries are far from the only businesses that generate toxic wastes. There is hardly any business, large or small, that does not generate at least some toxic wastes. The following are just a few of thousands of possible examples.

Local service stations pump fumes containing VOCs into the air as they pump gas into their customers' automobiles. Car repair garages generate a whole range of ignitable wastes, as well as large quantities of used lead-acid batteries. Dry cleaners are left with toxic residues in the filters of their dry-cleaning machines. Printing shops generate acids and bases and ink sludges that contain the heavy metals chromium and lead. Greenhouses use and discard a variety of toxic pesticides. Beauty shops discard wastes containing toxic cleaning solutions and solvents. Funeral parlors use hazardous chemicals, including formaldehyde, in preparing bodies for burial. Even artists generate toxic wastes in the form of used paints and dyes.

Those businesses that do not generate toxic wastes directly generate them indirectly. They use products that require the generation of toxic wastes during manufacture. By creating the demand for these products, they encourage the generation of more and more toxic wastes. What business does not use paper, for example? Paper production is directly responsible for many of the toxic effluents that are poured into the nation's waterways, including benzene. Even the production of this book will indirectly result in the generation of significant amounts of toxic wastes.

AGRICULTURE

A farm might seem an unlikely source of toxic wastes. When most of us think of a farm, they think of a healthy and wholesome place: of fresh air, clean streams, and rich fertile soil. Like most other businesses, however, modern farms use and eventually throw away significant amounts of toxic materials.

For one thing, farms use motorized machinery. Even a small modern farm might have a tractor, an electric generator, one or more pickup trucks, and various kinds of harvesting machines. These machines generate all the usual petroleum-related wastes, including waste oils and gasoline and exhaust fumes.

Most important, the majority of modern farms use large amounts of pesticides and chemical fertilizers. Not all pesticide wastes are considered toxic, but the EPA lists over 150 of them as hazardous. Among those classified as "acutely hazardous" are some of the most common brands of pesticides, including Aldicarb and Dinoseb.

Even disposing of the containers pesticides come in or those they are dispensed from is a serious waste management problem. There have been many cases of farm animals and even farmers being poisoned by pesticide residues in reused containers. One dairy farmer used an unwashed pesticide drum as a float in a pond on the farm. The next day, he found twenty cows who had drunk from the pond lying dead.

Used properly, most pesticides are considered "safe," both to the public and to the farmers who use them. But they are often not used safely. According to the Natural Resources Defense Counsel, a study of twenty-six fresh fruits and vegetables sold in American supermarkets showed that about one-half of them contained residues of dioxin, presumably from pesticides.

Used incorrectly or applied too heavily, pesticides and chemical fertilizers can seep down through the soil and into the groundwater. Once there, they contaminate the wells from which the farm families—and the people in the neighboring communities—get their drinking water.

In addition, wind and rain erosion wash pesticides and fertilizers into streams and rivers, poisoning the waters, killing fish and other aquatic life, entering the human food chain, and even threatening the health of swimmers.

Many pesticides used in agriculture are considered "hazardous" by the EPA. Residents living near this cotton field in Georgia complained that a pesticide sprayed by crop dusters had killed fish in the area. UPI/Bettmann Newsphotos

Even used correctly, nitrogen fertilizers can release significant amounts of nitrogen into the air. This nitrogen rises into the atmosphere and ultimately contributes to the destruction of the ozone layer.

Chemicals are not the only potentially dangerous wastes generated by farms. Animal wastes and even rotting plant wastes can be as harmful to parts of the environment as chemical wastes. Washed into waterways, they not only foul the waters but destroy the natural balance of life. By promoting the growth of bacteria, algae, and other plants, they can choke out other, higher forms of life in lakes, streams, and rivers.

MUNICIPAL SEWAGE SYSTEMS

Throughout history, sewage has been a threat to human health. Contamination of water supplies by sewage contributed to the plagues of ancient times. Although modern technological advances help to cut down on these kinds of risks, sewage disposal remains an important concern for virtually every community.

There are two distinct kinds of municipal sewage. The first is sludge, made up of human and other wastes flushed into the sewer system from toilets. The second is urban runoff, consisting of the many substances that get washed away from city streets by fallen rain. Carried by underground pipes called sanitary sewers, these wastes are usually treated at a wastewater treatment plant before being released into lakes, rivers, or oceans.

Properly treated, sludge presents no direct threat to human health. It can, however, present a threat to the natural balance of life in the waterways. Also, sewage treatment plants can break down or become overloaded. When they do, raw sewage can choke a river or threaten all the fish in a major lake. It can even affect the oceans. In recent summers, bathing beaches on both the Atlantic and Pacific coasts have been closed to swimmers because sewage was polluting the swimming areas and washing up on the shore.

Urban runoff can be even more of a problem. The mix of wastes in a typical sample of urban runoff might include soot, animal leavings, leaked oil and gasoline, solvents, road salts, particulates from air pollutants that have been brought down to earth by the rain, and even significant amounts of cadmium left on the pavement by wearing tires. Other major contaminants that are found in urban runoff include heavy metals, lead, copper, chromium, and zinc, as well as such deadly chemicals as lindane, chlordane, toulene, benzene, and PCBs.

Some cities have a single sewer system that carries both kinds of municipal wastes to a sewage treatment plant. Some release their storm sewer wastes directly into the nearest waterway without any treatment at all. At best, these effluents dirty the waterways that receive them. At worst, when the concentration of toxics is high enough, they poison them.

MEDICAL FACILITIES

Hospitals, laboratories, and other health facilities generate several kinds of toxic wastes, including leftover drugs and other chemicals, as well as human by-products that often contain germs or other contaminants that can cause disease. After a patient's blood has been tested for disease, the blood sample, whether healthy or diseased, becomes waste that has to be disposed of. The same is true of other bodily fluids and tissue samples. Even amputated body parts become wastes, sometimes contaminated by germs or disease.

The amount of hospital wastes has been mounting for decades. Because people are living to an older age and medical care is more widely available through government Medicare and Medicaid programs, the sheer number of hospital patients has grown over the years. Just as important, the amount of waste generated by the typical patient has been growing as well. The amount of hospital wastes per patient, per day, has doubled over the past fifty years.

Hospitals are not the only producers of medical wastes. Recent years have seen a great increase in the number of private clinics and medical laboratories. Each of these smaller institutions generates its own medical wastes.

The total amount of medical wastes is still small compared to the huge volume of wastes produced by either the manufacturing, mining, or farming industries. But medical wastes are becoming an increasing danger to human health.

This reality was brought home to many Americans in the summer of 1988, when large quantities of medical wastes washed up on public swimming beaches along the Atlantic coast. The wastes included used needles and vials of blood that were contaminated with the virus that causes the deadly and incurable disease AIDS (acquired immune deficiency syndrome)—a disease that is "caught" from just such contaminated blood. Before the summer was over, medical wastes had not only turned up on ocean beaches from Maine to North Carolina, but even on the shores of at least one of the Great Lakes.

It was not clear where all the medical wastes came from, but they were largely assumed to be the result of "midnight

In the summer of 1988, medical wastes dumped in New York coastal waters washed ashore, causing authorities to close many beaches, including this one on New York's Staten Island. Reuters/Bettmann Newsphotos

dumping" by hospitals. The public was shocked to learn that toxic medical wastes are routinely shipped out to sea and released into the oceans. According to toxic waste consultant Allen Hershkowitz, speaking in a Cable News Network television interview, it is even perfectly legal in many cities for infectious liquid wastes—including blood—to be simply flushed into the local sewage system. In New York City alone, Hershkowitz said, more than fifty hospitals have dumped infectious wastes either into the ocean or into the city's sewer system—or both.

THE MILITARY

Like any other big enterprise, the U.S. military generates its own toxic wastes. It is hard, however, to discover how much toxic waste the military actually produces and exactly how it is handled. Although the U.S. Navy quickly claimed responsibility for some of the medical wastes that washed up on North Carolina beaches in August 1988, that kind of admission is rare. Detailed information about radioactive wastes from nuclear weapons is usually shrouded in secrecy. Even information about other kinds of toxic waste disposal is often shrouded with secrecy.

There is suspicion, for instance, that the U.S. Army may have taken part in the dumping of some of the toxic chemicals at Love Canal. The chemical companies involved were military contractors, and residents of the area claimed that soldiers had helped with the disposal. When this charge was presented to the military, though, the Army flatly denied it. Later investigation by a New York State Assembly task force looking into the subject showed that the citizens may have been right.

CONSUMERS

The businesses and institutions discussed in this chapter do not generate all this toxic waste for themselves. They do it for us, the public. They do it because there is a demand—and sometimes a need—for the products and the services they provide.

As we have already seen, the family automobile is one of the major generators of several kinds of air pollutants, including carbon monoxide, carbon dioxide, and nitric oxide. As such, it is an important contributor to both acid rain and the greenhouse effect.

The typical modern American home is full of products whose manufacture requires the generation of toxic wastes, as well as substances that will soon become toxic wastes. These include detergents, cleaning fluids, nail polish and nail polish removers, insecticides, fungicides, fertilizers, rat and mouse poisons, furniture polishes, wood stains, wood preservatives, oven cleaners, toilet bowl cleaners, bleaches, ammonia, herbicides, disinfectants, paints and paint thinners, solvents, batteries, acids, expired prescription drugs, drain cleaners, waste oils, and used oil containers, along with some kinds of cosmetics, spot removers, expired patent medicines, rug and upholstery cleaners, aerosol cans, glass cleaners, air fresheners, glues, and a host of other common household items.

Many of these products are relatively harmless in the quantities in which they are found in the average home. When multiplied by the number of households in even a small city and building up over time in a dump or in a landfill, they can result in serious environmental hazards.

SO WHO IS TO BLAME?

The answer to the question that was asked at the beginning of this chapter is now clear: Who is to blame for the mountain of toxic waste that is towering over our country and the world? *We are.* All of us—the American public, along with the public of the rest of the developed world.

We are the ones who need the drugs, the lab tests, and the other medical services offered by the health care industry. We are the ones who demand the protection of the military and their nuclear weapons. We are the ones who demand the huge amounts of electricity that are generated by coal-burning and nuclear power plants. We are the ones who buy and eat the abundance of cheap food that is grown with the help of chemical fertilizers and pesticides. We are the ones who buy the millions of products produced by the automobile, petroleum, chemical, and other industries who generate the bulk of the toxic wastes spewed out in America today.

As the comic strip character, Pogo, once said, "We have met the enemy, and he is us."

CHAPTER SIX

DISPOSING OF

TOXIC WASTES

COMPANIES, cities, and other institutions have a number of options when disposing of toxic wastes. Each has advantages and disadvantages. Which one they choose depends on many factors, including the kind and amount of wastes involved.

LAND DISPOSAL

For most of human history, people have used the Earth as a gigantic garbage can. The easiest way of getting rid of garbage—toxic or otherwise—was simply to throw it away. That meant either tossing it on the surface of the ground or burying it underneath. So that's what most people did.

Mine tailings were simply piled up beside the huge holes from which they were dug. Unwanted chemicals, including solvents, medicines, and poisons of all kinds, were simply poured out onto the ground. In the big cities, all kinds of household wastes, from soapy water to the contents of chamber pots, were tossed out the windows of houses into the streets. Once the Industrial Revolution began, trash from factories, including worn-out machinery, was simply piled up behind the plant. City garbage was hauled to an open dump and left there to rot. If the dump was close to a center of population, the worst-smelling wastes were buried in order to keep them from stinking up the neighborhood.

The handling and treatment of toxic wastes has become more sophisticated in recent years, but the Earth is still often treated as a garbage can. In recent years, however, some innovative ways have been found to use the surface of the Earth to store or process wastes. One of the most interesting sewage treatment facilities in the country, for example, is an artificial wetland, built by the town of Arcadia, California. It acts as a kind of living filter for the town's raw sewage. This unique waste processor is not only effective in treating the sewage, it attracts wildlife—particularly wild birds—to the Arcadia area.

Despite such innovations, however, the most common way of using the earth to dispose of wastes is still to bury them in sites called "landfills."

SANITARY LANDFILLS

Sanitary landfills are made up of alternating layers of waste and dirt. First, a layer of waste is laid down, and compacted by a bulldozer. Then, a layer of dirt is spread over the waste, and it, too, is compacted. Another layer of refuse is compacted on top of the dirt, another layer on top of that, and so on.

Sanitary landfills are sometimes built in natural depressions in the Earth. These can be small hollows or valleys or even old mining pits. Sometimes, special holes or trenches are dug for the wastes. As layer after layer is added, however, the landfills rise above the surrounding ground, forming small, man-made hills.

The main advantage of sanitary landfills is the fact that they are relatively cheap and easy both to build and to operate. Most of the expense comes from buying the site and transporting the wastes to it. Another advantage is that once a landfill has been filled to capacity, the land over it can sometimes be used for other purposes. The city of Virginia Beach, Virginia, even uses a completed landfill—known as "Mount Trashmore"—as a park!

Many of the most dangerous of all the hazardous waste sites studied by the EPA are sanitary landfills. The most common danger associated with landfills is the threat to groundwater from leaching toxins. Another danger, however, comes from rotting organic wastes. Although these wastes are not toxic to begin with, the rotting process results in hazardous by-products in the form of methane gas and carbon dioxide. When trapped underground and confined under pressure in a landfill, these gases could explode.

Neither of these problems is impossible to deal with. Leaching can be cut down or eliminated by covering the bottom, sides, and top of the landfill with watertight materials. The danger from the buildup of gases can be solved by air vents that release the pressure.

Landfills that are carefully built and monitored to solve such problems in advance are known as "secure landfills." Even these have at least one remaining problem that cannot be completely solved. That is the fact that many buried wastes remain toxic, even underground. Long-lived chemical compounds, heavy metals, asbestos, and other toxic materials stay hazardous even when compacted and buried under the earth. There is always the risk that they will be disturbed someday and will return to harm the environment. In that sense, burial is always a temporary solution to the problem of toxic waste. Even in the most secure landfill, as a publication of the American Chemical

Society points out, "there is no guarantee that engineering solutions will be able to contain the wastes [forever]."

OCEAN DUMPING

As we have already seen, large amounts of municipal and industrial wastes are discharged into the nation's rivers. Additional toxic wastes enter streams and rivers through agricultural and urban runoff. Many of those wastes eventually find their way through the vast river systems and into one of the great oceans. Still other toxic wastes are dumped directly into the oceans by private companies and coastal communities.

If the Earth has been humanity's garbage can, the oceans were long mistakenly considered our natural waste treatment plants. Until recently, most people assumed that the oceans were indestructible, self-cleaning garbage disposals. No matter how much waste was thrown into them, it seemed, the oceans disposed of it with ease. Most of the wastes simply disappeared. They were eaten away by the fish or by the relentless actions of the churning saltwater itself. What was not actually destroyed was still sunk and gone forever, dwarfed by the vastness of the oceans. The oceans were so huge and so powerful that people simply could not imagine them ever becoming overloaded or wearing out. As a result, wastes of all kinds were—and still are—dumped at sea.

Evidence is growing, however, that the giant filters of the oceans are becoming clogged. In a sense, they never really existed. Most of the wastes dumped into the oceans were not really treated at all, as people had thought: They simply accumulated there. In any case, today, beluga whale carcasses that are declared hazardous waste sites, once fertile fishing areas where fish can no longer be found, sea crabs scrambling frantically ashore to escape the poisoned water—all these signs make clear that the oceans are not indestructible after all.

What's more, some of the wastes thrown into the oceans are returning to the shore. In recent summers, more and more beaches have had to be closed because of sewage and medical wastes contaminating the waters. In the summer of 1988—the hottest summer on record—most of the beaches of New Jersey, Long Island, and Rhode Island were deserted wastelands. Public health officials had closed them. That part of the Atlantic Ocean had become a toxic waste site. Yet the dumping of sewage and medical wastes into the oceans continued.

WIPP

The problem of nuclear wastes is still far from solved. Most importantly, there is still no permanent facility for the storage or treatment of high-level nuclear wastes. Finally, however, there is a plan for the "permanent" storage of at least the first generation of low-level radioactive wastes from nuclear power plants.

Up until now, the country's low-level nuclear wastes have been stored temporarily in fifty-five–gallon steel drums. These have been waiting, in a kind of warehouse, until a more stable site was found for them. At the time this book is being written, plans are under way for moving them to the first long-term depository. This storage facility, the Waste Isolation Pilot Project—or WIPP—was built by the Westinghouse company in the desert near the town of Carlsbad, New Mexico.

The wastes will be stored deep under the desert in a huge salt bed. When finished, the WIPP facility will be big enough to store billions of barrels of nuclear wastes from all over the country.

The barrels will eventually disintegrate, and the radioactive wastes will be released into the salt bed. The scientists and engineers who built the project believe that the salt will quickly seal in around the escaped wastes, trapping them safely deep underground. They claim that the salt formation is so stable that there is no danger the wastes will ever escape into the broader environment, even if the site is completely forgotten thousands of years from now. That kind of stability is necessary, since the wastes will remain radioactive for at least 10,000 years!

Critics of WIPP disagree. Ten thousand years, they point out, is a very long time. It is more than twenty times the amount of time that has passed since Columbus first sailed to North America. A lot can change in 10,000 years, they say, including the geology of the WIPP site.

Besides, they argue, any one of several possible disasters— from earthquakes to nuclear bombs—could break up the salt formation and allow the radioactive wastes to escape. Even without that kind of disaster, naturally occurring moisture could seep into and undermine the salt bed. Besides, they say, it will be extremely dangerous just to transport all the low-level nuclear wastes in the country to a single site. Every truck or train car carrying nuclear wastes across the country to New Mexico is a potential disaster waiting to happen.

Supporters of WIPP respond that there is no practical alternative. None of the possibilities raised by the critics, they say, is likely to occur. Besides, nuclear wastes already exist, and more are being generated all the time. They have to be put somewhere. However dangerous having one site may be, having many sites would only multiply the danger. While it may be conceivable that the New Mexico salt bed could be undermined by a natural or man-made disaster, it is the safest geologic formation that has yet been found.

DEEP-WELL INJECTION

Some liquid industrial wastes are disposed of by injecting them into the cracks and crevices of rock layers deep underground. A special kind of well is built to inject the wastes thousands of feet down into a layer of suitable rock.

When a porous layer of rock (one with holes or fractures) is completely surrounded by nonporous rocks, the porous rock can act as an effective container for the storage of liquid wastes. The rocks around it act as the walls of a well, enclosing the liquid and keeping it from leaching into the environment.

Nevertheless, the danger of groundwater contamination remains. The deep-well structure may simply leak over time, and both the wells and the surrounding rock layers are vulnerable to man-made shocks and natural disasters. A nearby explosion or earthquake could break them up and allow the liquids to escape. Because such rock formations are thousands of feet below the ground, it is difficult even to find out whether leaching is occurring.

In one recent year, only about 11 percent of all the hazardous wastes in the country were stored by deep-well injection. Most of them were acid solutions, petroleum-tainted water from oil-drilling operations, and liquid pulp wastes from paper mills— large-volume wastes that are a high risk to leach from ordinary land disposal sites.

INCINERATION

Some communities, as well as some private firms, burn at least part of their wastes. The combustion takes place in incinerators especially designed for the purpose. Many varieties of combustible solids, liquids, and gases can be at least partially disposed of in this way.

Incineration has the advantage of greatly reducing the total volume of wastes. In recent years, the typical municipal incinerator has reduced solid wastes by 85 to 90 percent. Future incineration will be even more efficient where toxic substances are involved. EPA standards now require that modern incineration units be capable of destroying or removing at least 99.99 percent of the toxic substances they treat.

Another advantage of incineration is that it destroys most, if not all, germs and other biological agents that could cause disease. For this reason, it is probably the best disposal method available for combustible medical wastes. Additionally, unlike landfills, incineration presents no immediate threat to the groundwater supply.

The disadvantages of incineration include the danger of air pollution. The combustion process inevitably involves the release of gases and particulates. In modern incinerators, however, a variety of filters, called "scrubbers," "scrub" the air containing the released materials. The filters trap most or all of these wastes before they can escape into the atmosphere. They are then added to the ash and other solid by-products of the combustion process and disposed of in some other way.

Another disadvantage of incineration is that its usefulness is limited to wastes that can be burned. It is not capable of disposing of heavy metals or explosive substances.

OTHER TREATMENTS

There are several other physical, chemical, biological, and thermal (or heat) processes that can be used to alter or destroy toxic wastes.

Physical Separation
The first step in disposing of some toxic wastes is to separate them from other substances with which they are combined. Toxic solids are separated from wastewater by several processes. Among the most common are sedimentation, in which the solid is allowed to sink to the bottom; evaporation, in which the water is simply evaporated away, leaving the toxic substance behind; and filtration, in which the wastewater is run through a filter or membrane to trap the toxic materials while allowing the rest of the liquid to pass through. Once the toxic substances have been separated, of course, they still have to be disposed of by some other method.

Microbiological Treatments

Some kinds of organic wastes, like sewage, can be made harmless by tiny living organisms called "microbes." The microbes "eat" the wastes for their own nourishment. In doing so, they break the toxic wastes down into molecules of the relatively harmless substances that made up the wastes. This process is sometimes called "biodegradation."

The most familiar form of biodegradation is composting, in which microbes turn nontoxic wastes, like leaves, grass clippings, and paper, into a natural fertilizer for gardens.

Biodegradation is primarily useful for disposing of organic wastes like sewage. It has the disadvantage of requiring some form of physical separation or pretreatment of the waste before it can be used. Additionally, some microbiological treatments have the disadvantage of taking up relatively large amounts of space and requiring relatively long periods of time to work.

Fixation

Fixation processes convert unstable wastes into more solid, less mobile forms. They are often used on wastes that tend to break up easily or that dissolve in water. Fixing them lessens the possibility that they will leach from a landfill or other disposal site into the groundwater.

Some fixation processes involve combining toxic materials with nontoxic substances that bind them into a solid brick or pellet. Some enclose the wastes in a kind of protective capsule. Although fixation doesn't make the substances themselves less toxic, it lessens their ability to escape into the environment. It also can be used to make wastes easier and safer to transport.

Chemical Processes

There are a number of ways that different chemical processes can be used to dispose of toxic wastes. Toxic acids can be neutralized by mixing them with bases, while toxic bases can be neutralized by mixing them with acids. This breaks them up, transforming them into salts and water. This form of neutraliza-

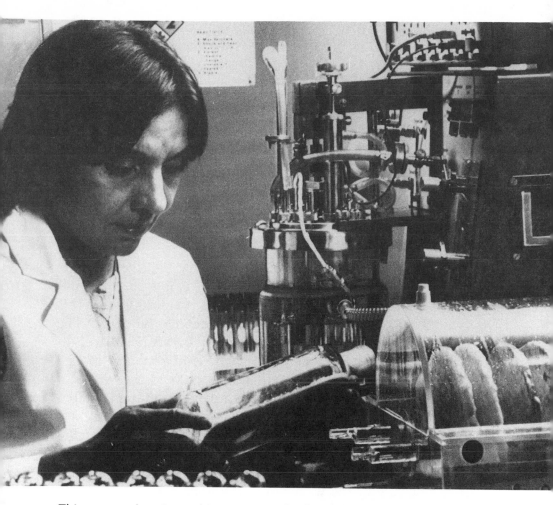

This researcher is seeking new methods of degrading hazardous wastes with organic materials. AP/Wide World Photos

tion is often used to treat acid and alkaline wastes from metal-processing procedures. Sometimes, toxic acids actually can be blended with toxic alkalines in a way that renders both of them harmless.

Heavy metals can be removed from a liquid solution by passing the liquid through an organic substance known as a "resin." The inorganic metals exchange ions with the resin, in a sense trapping the metals there. The metals then can be easily removed from the resin, then reused, stored, or disposed of in some other way. This process is typically used to remove mercury, barium, or lead from contaminated water.

A category of chemical reactions called "redox" can be used to break up the chemical bonds that hold certain kinds of hydrocarbons, sulphur compounds, and cyanide-contaminated wastewater together.

RECYCLING

Many toxic wastes can be recycled. That is, they can be collected, reprocessed, and used again. This is true, for example, of several kinds of metals. Almost half the lead used in this country is recycled and about 24 percent of the silver. The recycling of aluminum cans is becoming commonplace. In addition, some used solvents and petroleum products can be collected, purified or rerefined, and put back to use.

Recycling saves resources by using them again, and it often saves time, money, and energy as well. Perhaps the most important reason for recycling is that it cuts down on the total amount of toxic wastes. It does this directly, of course, by recovering materials that would otherwise become toxic wastes. It cuts down on toxic wastes in indirect ways, too.

Plants that recycle paper, for example, generage much less toxic waste than the paper mills that produced the paper in the first place. (In addition, by saving forest resources, recycling paper helps improve the planet's capacity for handling carbon dioxide.) In the same way, recycling metals almost always produces fewer toxic wastes than would be produced by mining and refining fresh supplies of metals to replace them.

The reduction in wastes can be dramatic. Recycling scrap iron, for example, results in only 14 percent of the air pollution and 24 percent of the water pollution that a steel mill generates producing the same amount of iron from ore. In addition, recycling processes often use significantly less energy than

A recycling process converted industrial wastes, including hazardous materials, into this environmentally safe slag. The slag is used in the construction of roads and in other building projects. AP/Wide World Photos

original production processes do. This means less of the toxic wastes associated with energy production as well.

CONVERSION

Instead of simply being recycled, it is possible to transform some kinds of toxic wastes into new products with entirely different uses. This is called "conversion." Several communities have experimented with conversion of sewage sludge. Chicago and Philadelphia, for example, have used fixation processes to turn their sewage sludge into fertilizer pellets for farmlands. Others have turned sludge into solid bricks and other building materials. Richland, Washington, has a plant that turns sludge into #4 diesel oil.

Some kinds of wastes can be converted into valuable energy. Some communities turn the problem—and the danger—presented by the methane gas buildup in secure landfills into a benefit. They trap the methane gas and use it as fuel. One city in Nassau County, New York, harnesses the energy from its municipal incinerator and uses it to generate electricity. It saves about $700,000 a year by burning its wastes in this way.

NEW TECHNOLOGIES

Many researchers are busy working on new waste treatment technologies for the future. Some are merely improvements on the processes already in use. Others are new. Several companies are working on a device they call a "plasma torch." It works by atomizing toxic chemical compounds and breaking them down into basic elements like nitrogen and oxygen. Westinghouse Corporation plans to experiment with this kind of device on the toxic "stew" that still remains at Love Canal.

Scientists have found that some ordinarily indissoluble toxic chemicals can be dissolved by submerging them in water at high temperatures under extremely high pressure. When oxygen is added to this compressed and heated water, it oxidizes the chemicals and transforms them into carbon dioxide and water.

In the field of biodegradation, work is being done with microbes that will attack inorganic, as well as organic, chemicals. This means that microbiological treatment soon may be widely used to break down a whole new range of toxic substances. Microbes already have been used to help dispose of major oil spills.

Thought has even been given to the possibility of using rocket ships to send some of the most deadly toxic wastes—particularly radioactive wastes—into space. Some scientists scoff at this proposal, saying that it is irresponsible, as well as economically inefficient. Others think it holds the best long-term hope for "safe" disposal of high-level radioactive wastes.

Some of these new technologies already are being used on a small scale. Others are under development. Some will almost certainly prove to be ineffective, unreliable, or uneconomic. Some, though, will almost certainly provide useful new directions for the future.

CHAPTER SEVEN

MAKING
THE RULES—
GOVERNMENT
REGULATION

DECIDING which method to use in disposing of toxic wastes is a complicated procedure. The American Chemical Society's publication, *Hazardous Waste Management*, suggests thirty-three different questions companies should ask when deciding how to get rid of their toxic wastes.

The questions provide a key to the wide range of important scientific, technical, environmental, social, economic, and regulatory considerations that have to be taken into account. They include, "What are the technologies that are practical for each waste type?" "Is the equipment overly complex, susceptible to breakdown, or difficult to repair?" "What forms of energy are required to run the facility?" "How will the technology affect the local job market?" "Is pretreatment of the waste necessary?" "How reliable is the technology for consistent performance over time?" "If the technology fails, how severe will the contamination be?" "Who will monitor the facility and how?" "What happens if the company goes bankrupt or is purchased by another owner?" "Are there opportunities for energy or material recovery for resale?"

Throughout American history, most of the companies and institutions that produced toxic wastes didn't bother with environmental and social questions at all. Only the economic considerations would have been taken into account. With no outside pressure demanding that they consider public health and safety, most companies simply chose the cheapest waste disposal method they could find.

Even those generators who *did* worry about the public safety tried to strike a balance between society's interests and those of their company. They were willing to spend more than they absolutely had to spend in order to protect public health and safety, but only a limited amount more. Very few companies or even governmental institutions believed that they had the responsibility for protecting the public from the toxic wastes they produced—not, at least, if it would cost them a lot of money to do so.

A 1970 *Wall Street Journal* survey reported that more than 40 percent of 1,372 companies surveyed spent only 1 percent or less on pollution control. Nonetheless, many business executives were convinced that pollution control was already costing their companies more than the companies could afford to spend. Believing this, it is not surprising that few businesses chose waste disposal methods that truly protected the public. Still another American Management Association (AMA) survey in the early 1970s revealed that less than half of companies polled were even keeping track of how much toxic waste they were generating.

The great majority of companies relied on the least secure means of disposing of their wastes. Fifty-eight percent, for example, depended on landfills. Nineteen percent dumped most of their wastes into rivers, 4 percent into the local sewer system, and 3 percent into the ocean. Safer and more permanent alternatives—like oxidation, neutralization, recycling, and reprocessing—were chosen as the main means of disposal by only 1 percent of the 236 companies who responded.

Even some business executives were becoming aware they were not living up to their social responsibilities. As one told the American Management Association in 1972: "Too long have we lived like slobs—dumping our trash out for someone else to cope with."

Most business executives, however, seemed determined to ignore or deny the problem. It was becoming clear to many health authorities and environmentalists that some sort of pressure was going to be needed if businesses were going to stop behaving like "slobs." The most logical source of that pressure was government. By the late 1960s, some states had already begun to pass strict anti-pollution laws. Some of those state laws—especially the California laws regulating air pollution— would become models for future federal legislation.

The state regulation, by itself, was not effective. While a few states had effective laws regulating some kinds of wastes, many other states had few laws or no laws at all. Even the most effective state laws could only be effective within that state's borders. Serious polluters always had the ability simply to move their operations from a state with strict laws to a state with no laws at all.

If businesses would not do the job themselves and state regulation was ineffective, what should be done? Another business executive quizzed by the AMA suggested the obvious answer: "[The] federal government should gradually, but forcefully, tighten the noose on everyone to protect future generations." Most environmentalists agreed. The federal government, however, was reluctant to act.

A RELUCTANT GOVERNMENT

Toxic wastes had been piling up in the United States more than two centuries before the federal government took its first halting steps toward regulating them. There were several reasons the government was so slow to act.

Philosophically, many conservative politicians were convinced that environmental concerns, like toxic wastes, were none of the government's business. Private companies generated most of the toxic wastes, they maintained, and private companies should decide how to dispose of them.

Politically, toxic wastes have not been a popular issue. In a representative democracy like ours, government action tends to follow, instead of lead, public opinion. Congress is particularly reluctant to take any action opposed by powerful political or economic forces of any kind unless there are equal or more powerful forces on the other side.

When it came to the issue of toxic wastes, most of the power, and almost all of the money, was lined up against regulation. The chemical, mining, and other industries that generated most of the toxic wastes were strongly opposed. Those industries worried that government regulations would require them to spend large amounts of money on pollution control and waste treatment equipment: money that would cut into their profits. They used their resources to convince both the politicians and the public at large that there was no need for pollution control or waste treatment. Company leaders argued that they knew better than any government official how to run their companies in the most efficient, profitable, and safe way.

In any case, company officials argued, government regulation was pointless. Toxic wastes were not a serious threat to the public. They insisted that many of the wastes involved were not nearly as dangerous as environmentalists claimed. When it came to the wastes that really *were* dangerous, companies claimed that they were taking every reasonable precaution already. There was no reason for the government to police private industry: It was already policing itself.

To support their arguments, industry leaders brought out statistics showing that people were living longer than ever before. Back in the eighteenth century, they argued, most of the babies born in the United States couldn't expect to live to be adults. That was long before toxic wastes were a serious problem. By 1920, however—long after the Industrial Revolution had begun spewing out its tons of new toxic wastes—the average American baby could expect to live to age fifty-four. By the 1960s, when the generation of toxic wastes was skyrocketing, Americans could expect to live to be seventy years old. Didn't these statistics alone prove that toxic wastes were not a serious threat to public health? If those wastes were poisoning the public, as the environmentalists claimed, shouldn't life expectancy be going down instead of up?

Although the forces opposed to government action were powerful and well funded, the environmentalists were relatively unorganized and underfunded. The forces arrayed against the powerful industries that opposed regulation represented a wide variety of interests and concerns.

Environmentalism grew up at a time when many people were beginning to protest American activities at home and abroad. Some of the environmentalists were protesters, who saw the polluting industries as part of the same "power structure" that supported racial discrimination and American involvement in Vietnam. Some were scientists, who were primarily concerned with long-term issues like acid rain, threats to the ozone layer, and the greenhouse effect. Others were doctors, worried about the effects of toxic wastes on people's health. Still others were simply conservationists, people who loved the beauty of the outdoors and hoped to preserve it.

The environmentalists protested that the industries' life expectancy statistics were irrelevant. They said that new wonder drugs, advances in medical procedures, and improvements in hygiene and nutrition were the reasons most Americans were living longer. The environmentalists argued that the rise in life expectancy probably would have been even greater if it had not been for the growing menace of toxic wastes.

The environmentalists were convinced that toxic wastes were a national problem. A national problem, they believed, needed national solutions. That meant federal government regulation of toxic wastes.

The environmentalists were well meaning, but they lacked the money and political clout of the industries that opposed them. If the environmentalists were to overcome the influence of their opponents, they would have to get public opinion strongly behind them. They had one powerful ally in that effort: fear—a growing public concern about the dangers of toxic wastes.

EARLY REGULATION

The first federal regulation of toxic wastes was the revised Atomic Energy Act of 1954. That date was surprisingly early because it was long before the environmental movement really got started. What was not surprising was that the wastes the Act regulated were the wastes the public was already most frightened of: atomic, or nuclear, wastes.

Atomic power was new in 1954, and most Americans were already frightened by it. In the public mind, it was not only associated with the vast destructive force of the atomic bomb, but with the even more frightening mystery of deadly radiation. (Several popular movies of the 1950s dealt with evil monsters that had been somehow created by exposure to radioactive wastes.) That public concern helped ensure that the revised Atomic Energy Act of 1954 called for some regulation of the disposal of low-level radioactive wastes in water.

A year later, the first federal law dealing with air pollution was passed. It was not, however, a regulatory bill. It only called for research into the problem of air pollution by the U.S. Public Health Service. It wasn't until a decade later that the Clean Air Act of 1963 provided funds for more research and offered some federal support to state programs designed to improve the quality of the air. Two years later, the Act was amended to set the first national standards for the amounts of air pollutants to be allowed in automobile exhausts.

Also in 1965, Congress passed the first federal law primarily designed to deal with the problem of solid wastes: the Solid Waste Disposal Act of 1965. It was a weak bill. It called for research, not for regulation, and only dealt with solid wastes in general, giving no special attention to toxic wastes as such. It did not even make a distinction between industrial wastes and household garbage. Still, it was a start.

A DECADE OF PROGRESS

The key year in the history of toxic waste control in the United States was 1970. It was the year that the environmental movement demonstrated that it had come of age as an important political force; and it was the year that the federal government finally began to commit to a real role in the management of toxic wastes.

It was on April 22, 1970, that American environmentalists declared the first celebration of Earth Day. From New York to San Francisco, they held rallies to call attention to the dangers of pollution. The crowds that turned out for these combination protests and celebrations dwarfed any previous environmental demonstrations in the United States.

Unlike the civil rights and antiwar demonstrations of the 1960s, the Earth Day rallies were welcomed by the public authorities in many of the communities where they were held. Even many of the people who didn't participate in the events sympathized with the cause. A part of New York's fashionable Fifth Avenue was closed for one demonstration. In Washington, D.C., Congress adjourned in honor of Earth Day. Estimates of the number of people who participated in the nationwide demonstrations ranged into the millions. It was clear that a concern about the future of the environment and worry about toxic wastes were no longer confined to a few fringe groups in the society. Environmentalism had become a popular cause.

The effects of the changing public attitude soon brought

On Earth Day, 1970, junior high school students in St. Louis, Missouri, protested against pollution and smog caused by fumes from automobile exhaust. UPI/Bettmann Newsphotos

about a host of new federal laws. A new Solid Waste Act was passed that year. Although it stopped short of providing actual federal regulation, it called for research into the specific problems associated with dangerous wastes. More important, a series of tough new amendments was added to the Clean Air Act in 1970. Most important of all, the U.S. Environmental Protection Agency was established.

Nineteen seventy proved to be the start of a decade of growing federal involvement in pollution control generally, and toxic waste control in particular. Within a few years, a wide range of polluting activities were brought under federal regulation for the first time.

In 1972, a new Clean Water Act regulated all hazardous wastes "discharged into navigable waters" within the United States. It called for the end to all such dumping by 1985. Also in 1972, the Marine Protection Research and Sanctuaries Act began the regulation of ocean dumping, and the Insecticide, Fungicide, and Rodenticide Act brought pesticides under federal control. That same year saw the shipping of oil regulated under the Ports and Waterways Safety Act. In 1974, the Hazardous Materials Transportation Act brought truck and rail movement of toxic wastes under federal regulation as well.

THE RESOURCE CONSERVATION AND RECOVERY ACT

The most far reaching of all the environmental acts passed in the 1970s was the Resource Conservation and Recovery Act of 1976, known as RCRA. To this day, RCRA serves as the basic law regulating toxic waste management in the United States. Actually a complex series of regulations and requirements dealing with toxic wastes, RCRA is administered by the Environmental Protection Agency.

An extremely ambitious program, RCRA is intended to do more than just contain dangerous wastes. It established a "cradle to grave" system designed to control the manufacture and use of dangerous substances, as well as their final disposal, in ways that will benefit the environment.

In the words of a Congressional Research Service Issue Brief prepared by James E. MacCarthy, RCRA "sought to establish a framework that would lead to the recovery of waste resources and the proper disposal of all remaining residues. Resource recovery was to be fostered through research, development, and other activities."

The states were to be involved as well. The federal government was to "financially [assist them] to set up their own comprehensive planning and waste control agencies." By January 1988, most of the states had taken over the management of at least parts of the RCRA program within their borders.

Under RCRA, the EPA is required to identify potential toxic wastes long before they become wastes—in some cases, before they are even manufactured. It is then obliged to see that the businesses that manufacture and use potential waste products handle them properly. Specific standards are set for the owners and operators of TSDs, which means all facilities that treat, store, or dispose of toxic wastes. New TSDs must show that they meet those standards before they can be licensed. Existing operations can continue under "interim status" until their applications for permits have been either accepted or rejected. Licensed TSDs eventually will be required to eliminate 99.9 percent of all the toxic wastes they treat.

Ultimately, RCRA's proclaimed goal is to have no more toxic wastes at all. Some observers consider this an unlikely and maybe even impossible goal. If it is to be met, it is clear that many new technologies, like those discussed in Chapter 6, will be necessary. Unless at least some of them prove effective and on a much larger scale than they have been used so far, it is hard to see how toxic wastes can be eliminated altogether from our environment.

CHANGES IN BUSINESS ATTITUDES

The great changes in public sentiment since the 1950s, as well as increased government regulation, have had great effects on the business community.

In the early 1970s, more than 40 percent of the companies who responded to a *Wall St. Journal* poll reported that they spent less than 1 percent of their income on pollution control of all kinds. At almost the same time, another survey reported that about the same percentage of business executives felt they were already spending so much that their company was in financial danger because of it. Yet businesses today are spending much more than they used to on disposing of toxic wastes more safely, and most are at least as healthy financially as they were in the 1970s.

Partly, of course, they are spending more because government regulations force them to do it. Partly, though, the increased spending reflects a change in attitude among many business executives.

In the 1960s and early 1970s, most business executives placed a relatively low priority on their responsibility to society. In an AMA survey at the time, executives were asked to rank several objectives on a scale of 1 to 6. Even though they could give a number one priority to as many objectives as they wanted to, only 23 percent of the executives ranked "social responsibilities" as high as number two. At the same time, 83 percent of the same executives ranked profits number one, while all the others ranked it number two.

Although we have no comparable recent survey, it's unlikely that so few executives would give a high priority to social responsibilities today. Certainly few executives would dare to claim that they have no responsibility to protect the public from the toxic wastes their companies produce. Publicly, at least, most businessmen acknowledge that they have a moral responsibility to protect the public as much as possible.

THE 1980s

The fact that more business executives are willing to acknowledge their responsibility to dispose of their wastes safely doesn't mean that they are living up to it. In fact, the rapid progress of the 1970s slowed down dramatically in the 1980s.

As we will see more clearly in the next chapter, part of the reason for this slowdown was the attitude of the presidential administration of Ronald Reagan (1981-1989). The president was suspicious and even hostile toward federal regulation of industry. The people he put in charge of the EPA and other government agencies were often hostile as well. As a result, the federal environmental agencies moved only slowly (and, it seemed to many critics, reluctantly) to impose regulations on the producers and handlers of toxic wastes.

Congress tried to force faster action in 1984 by adding several Hazardous and Solid Waste Amendments (HSWA) to RCRA. The most important of them imposed "hammers"—penalties against TSDs that refused to meet RCRA's requirements.

Because EPA has been very slow to act on land disposal permits, one of the amendments required even TSDs operating an interim status to meet at least two RCRA requirements. They must monitor effects on nearby groundwater and they must prove that they have sufficient resources to meet their likely financial obligations under the regulations. So far, less than one third of the land disposal TSDs have shown that they can meet those standards. Some have been closed down.

The EPA's slowness causes problems for the TSDs as well. Under RCRA and HSWA, it was given the job of establishing a wide variety of new regulations for TSDs and hazardous waste generators alike: regulations designed to ensure the elimination of 99.9 percent of all toxic wastes. Many of the necessary regulations, however, have not even been formulated yet. TSDs, therefore, have no way of knowing what requirements they may be asked to meet in the future.

A recent study conducted by the Environmental and Energy Study Institute criticized the EPA for its lack of clear policies. According to the study:

> Uncertainty about whether and when the restrictions will be enforced is producing a widespread "wait and see" attitude among hazardous waste generators, commercial waste treatment firms, and state regulators. Generators don't know when they will have to comply with the restrictions, commercial firms are not sure when they will need additional capacity, and state regulators don't know what to tell the regulatory industry, or whether to gear up to enforce the restrictions.

As a result, the study complains, "land disposal appears likely to continue to a much greater extent than intended by Congress, posing continued threats to ground and surface waters and public health." Senator Bill Bradley of New Jersey and other congressional critics agree. They complain, in Bradley's words, that the EPA has simply "not been doing its job."

By mid-1988, twelve years after the passage of RCRA, only 598 of the more than 4,000 TSD facilities in the United States had gotten permits from either EPA or the states. Eighty-six others had been denied permits and ordered to close. All the rest were still operating under the relatively easy interim status rules.

However successful the measures discussed in this chapter may be in the future, there is a more immediate problem to solve. That is the mountain of toxic waste we already have.

CHAPTER EIGHT

CLEANING UP

THE MESS

THE Love Canal tragedy brought the problem of the nation's already existing toxic waste sites to national attention. Congress attempted to do something about them by passing the Comprehensive Environmental Relief, Compensation and Liability Act of 1980. Known as "CERCLA" for short, it was intended to promote the nation's ability to manage, treat, and dispose of toxic wastes in every way possible. Its most immediate goal was to see that hazardous waste sites like the one at Love Canal were cleaned up.

CERCLA directed the EPA to identify and study all existing toxic waste sites. The agency was to decide which of the sites were the most dangerous and needed the most immediate action and then ensure that they were cleaned up as soon as possible.

A $1.6 billion hazardous waste trust fund was set up to allow the EPA to do its job. This so-called Superfund was to be supported by taxes on industries, such as oil and chemicals, that produced large amounts of toxic wastes.

As big as Superfund was, however, it was nowhere near big enough to pay for cleaning up all the hazardous waste sites in the United States. A consulting firm, hired by the EPA, estimated then that it would take at least $45 billion to do the job. Most estimates today are at least $100 billion.

But Congress never intended Superfund to pay the bill. Congress ordered that, where possible, the companies that had contaminated the sites in the first place should pay for cleaning them up. The EPA was given authority to order polluters to clean up the sites, and it had the authority to go to court to enforce its orders if necessary. This principle—that the polluter should pay—has been called the "cornerstone" of the entire CERCLA program.

The money in Superfund was only to be used for two purposes. The first was to clean up dangerous sites whose owners could not be made to pay. These included sites where the polluters could not be identified, or were dead, or had gone out of business. Second, Superfund money was to be available to meet any sudden emergencies involving toxic substances.

Whenever Superfund money *was* used, it was to be matched by money from the states in which the sites were located. The states were to pay 10 percent of the costs at a site that was privately owned and 50 percent if it was owned by a state or local government.

HOW THE SUPERFUND PROGRAM WORKS

There are several steps involved in the cleanup of a typical Superfund site. The first is identification of the site by the EPA.

This sometimes comes about by the voluntary reporting by the operator of the site, who is required to report conditions there to the EPA. In the case of "midnight dumping" or abandoned sites, the site may be reported by concerned citizens who suspect the existence of the site. Local officials may also discover a site in the course of their duties.

Once the EPA is informed of a possibly dangerous site, it investigates. It finds out how big the site is, what toxic substances are deposited there, and how dangerous they may be to the environment. The EPA also takes into account the geography of the area and the nearness of the site to both surface water and groundwater and to human and animal populations.

An actual visit is then sometimes made to the site and samples taken of any chemicals found, as well as of nearby soils and water. If signs of danger are found, a check is made to see whether the site is in an area visited by children.

If these investigations uncover a potential emergency—poisons already leaking into a drinking water supply, for instance, or chemicals in danger of blowing up—the EPA may carry out a removal. Removals are emergency actions, designed to eliminate a short-term threat to safety.

If the threat presented by a particular site is high enough, the site is given a rank on the national priorities list. This is a list of those toxic waste sites eligible for a Superfund cleanup.

Among the factors considered in ranking a site on the list are the toxicity and amount of the hazardous substances present, the likelihood that they will escape into the environment, how far contamination might spread, and how many people are likely to be exposed to danger.

Once the site has been inspected and ranked, a remedial investigation is done. This is designed to determine the best way to remedy the problem and clean up the site. This remedial investigation is used as the basis for a record of decision, or ROD. The ROD is the official selection of the method that will ultimately be used to clean up the site.

This unfenced, unmarked land on the outskirts of Denver, Colorado, was occupied by a chemical company that burned in 1965. In the 1980s, it was declared a toxic waste site and placed on the EPA's priorities list. UPI/Bettmann Newsphotos

CONTROVERSY OVER SUPERFUND

The Superfund program has been plagued by controversy from the start. The first years of Superfund were also the first years of the presidential administration of Ronald Reagan. There was a strong feeling among supporters of the Superfund idea in Congress that the Reagan administration was fundamentally hostile to it. They felt that the president had deliberately put opponents of Superfund in charge of the EPA, which administered it. Environmentalists and critics in Congress were soon charging that these unsympathetic administrators were destroying the program from within.

The conflict between the EPA-Superfund administrators and Congress quickly turned into a scandal. In 1982, Anne Gorsuch, the Reagan appointee who headed the EPA, refused to turn over documents to a congressional committee. Angry committee members made her the first cabinet level officer in history to be cited for contempt of Congress. A year later, Rita Lavelle, the EPA official in charge of the Superfund was found guilty of perjury for lying to Congress.

By the mid-1980s, environmentalists were upset with the snail-like progress of the Superfund. Six years after the program had been authorized, only 14 of the nearly 900 sites then on the national priorities list had been cleaned up.

The EPA admitted that progress on actual Superfund cleanups had been slow. They insisted that it was not the EPA's fault. In the words of one EPA publication:

> Completion of cleanups has proved more difficult and more time-consuming than anyone at first imagined: This has been particularly true of NPL [national priorities list] sites, which rank as the worst in the nation. It has been estimated that EPA-managed cleanups under the Superfund program require an average of 5.54 calendar years from start to finish. Completions will be more frequent in years to come as work proceeds at sites where preliminary cleanup stages have already been completed.

In the meantime, the EPA insisted that the agency had been far from idle. More than 20,000 potentially dangerous sites had been given at least a preliminary assessment. Some 6,484 of them had already been identified as possible threats to health or the environment, and the 888 most dangerous had been slated to be placed on the national priorities list.

Although it was true that only 14 sites had been removed from the national priorities list, cleanups were in progress at 156 other sites. Settlement agreements had been reached at 372 sites, and there had been emergency removal actions at 716 others. Civil court actions had been initiated against polluters at 91 sites, and the EPA had issued administrative orders, directing potential polluters to take action to prevent future contamination, at more than 400 others. In addition, the EPA had collected more than $650 million from polluters, actually increasing the size of the Superfund over the first six years of its existence.

Whether the congressional suspicions of the EPA were justified or not, Congress was not satisfied with Superfund's progress. It moved to strengthen the program with SARA—the Superfund Amendments and Reauthorization Act of 1986.

SARA

Perhaps the single most important feature of SARA was a major change in definition. Originally CERCLA had been vague about exactly what "cleaning up" a hazardous waste site meant. The EPA adopted what has been called the "least cost technologically achievable remedy" definition. In deciding how to approach the job of cleaning up a site, the EPA balanced the cost of various cleanup methods against their effectiveness. It looked for the cheapest way of cleaning up the site, even if that way was not the most effective. SARA directed a change in the EPA's priorities. It ordered the EPA to choose only the least expensive way that would achieve a "permanent remedy." This change in definition was really a change in philosophy.

Take a case of leaking storage drums found buried in a landfill. One option might be to seal up the leaks in the drums themselves. This would have the advantage of being relatively cheap to do, but it would have the disadvantage of being temporary. Eventually the drum will deteriorate again, and the toxic chemicals will escape.

The second option would be to remove the drums, incinerate their contents, and decontaminate the landfill. This would be many times more expensive, but it would have the advantage of being a permanent solution to the problem.

Under the original Act, the EPA could choose the first, the cheaper but short-sighted solution. Since SARA, however, the EPA is required to choose the second, the permanent solution.

In passing SARA, Congress gave Superfund some powerful new weapons in its battle against toxic wastes. The first and most dramatic of these weapons was more money. The original Superfund contained $1.6 billion. Under SARA, the trust fund was extended to a staggering $8.5 billion. Along with the increased trust fund, limits on how much specific Superfund removals (and other activities) could cost were raised.

In addition, SARA increased EPA's power to make and enforce settlement agreements with polluters. To give the EPA more information, it set criminal penalties for polluters who refused to supply details on discharges of toxic wastes or who gave the agency false information.

SARA also established a major new research and development program to help develop better technologies for disposing of toxic wastes in the future. New training programs were started as well to prepare people to respond to toxic waste problems and emergencies.

SARA didn't just give the EPA new weapons—it ordered the agency to use them. It attempted to speed up the EPA by establishing goals, timetables, and deadlines for the agency. These included goals for completing preliminary assessments to decide which sites belonged on the national priorities list. In addition, SARA ordered that at least 275 remedial studies and investigations be completed by 1989 and that at least 175 others be in their final stages by that time, with 200 more by 1991.

During Superfund's early years, critics often complained about the ways Superfund cleanups were carried out. Too often, they said, the cleanups were slapdash, or done in ways that only changed the nature of the danger instead of eliminating it.

Among other things, critics charged that some of the EPA's emergency removal actions had actually made later permanent cleanup of the sites more difficult. SARA directed that future Superfund removals be carried out in ways that contributed to long-term remedial actions.

Additionally, SARA ordered that permanent cleanups be consistent with state and federal pollution laws. All the wastes removed from a Superfund site to be stored elsewhere had to be taken to sites that met the RCRA standards.

SARA also moved to make toxic waste management more democratic. Its Title III orders all handlers of toxic wastes to make detailed reports of any accidents or other dangerous situations involving toxic wastes. Releases describing accidents are to be sent to the news media to make sure that the information is made public. If enforced, this requirement will do much to break down the secrecy that surrounded the disposal of toxic wastes at places like Love Canal.

GRADING THE SUPERFUND

The House Oversight and Investigations Committee held hearings in 1988 to evaluate the Superfund's performance under SARA. Members promised Superfund's recent record of removals. The agency had carried out 315 of the emergency operations since the passage of SARA. The comittee also heard stinging criticism of Superfund and its EPA administrators from witnesses concerned with the environment.

One of the most critical witnesses was Richard Fortuna, director of the Hazardous Waste Treatment Council, an association of high-technology firms specializing in the treatment of toxic wastes. Along with six environmental groups, the council prepared a study of all the 1987 RODs. In their study, the groups had set out to praise the decisions that were good for the environment, as well as to criticize those that were bad. In Fortuna's words, they were looking for "the good, the bad, and

Today, Americans are well informed about the dangers of toxic wastes. This public awareness has led citizens such as these New Jersey residents to protest the location of toxic waste storage facilities in their communities. UPI/Bettmann Newsphotos

the ugly." What they found, he said, was "some good decisions, many bad, and several downright ugly decisions."

According to Fortuna, there was "little evidence that SARA was ever passed." Instead of trying to clean up the sites permanently, he testified, the EPA usually settled for half-baked, temporary solutions. Only six of the seventy-five RODs handed down in 1987 involved a "credible attempt to institute a permanent solution" to the contamination at the site. Of the

91

rest, 68 percent involved no treatment of the principal source of the contamination at all. The other 24 percent involved only "token treatment," or treatment that even the EPA admitted was ineffective. The temporary measures of "capping" or "containment" were still the main methods by which the EPA was dealing with toxic waste sites.

A. Blakeman Early, of the environmentalist Sierra Club, was even more critical than Fortuna. "Superfund," he said, "is clearly a train that is out of control and charging down the wrong track." Early was especially harsh in his criticism of the way EPA set goals for Superfund cleanups. In SARA, Congress had directed the EPA to set the strictest cleanup goals possible. In all of 1987, according to Early, the EPA had only required the maximum possible cleanup of a site in one case. In many others, it had set no specific cleanup requirements at all.

In still other cases, the EPA had set goals that were wildly inconsistent with each other. Early gave examples of limits set for groundwater contamination by the deadly chemical benzene. At one site, he claimed, the allowable level of benzene had been set 30 times lower than at another site. At a third site, it had been set almost 100 times lower. Early suggested that in setting such contradictory standards, the EPA seemed to be "using the practical equivalent of a dart board."

The witnesses leveled a variety of charges against the EPA, ranging from poor management decisions to complete incompetence. The agency had sometimes rejected new waste treatment technologies as too expensive before taking bids to find out how much they would actually cost. In one case, it was said, the EPA had deliberately inflated its estimates of what one disposal method would cost by 1,500 percent in order to use the high estimate as a reason for rejecting it. In another, the EPA had set a removal level of "visible contamination" for PCBs—chemicals that are colorless and therefore *in*visible to begin with.

Some members of the committee were especially concerned by what seemed to be EPA's reluctance to force polluters to pay for cleanups. Representative Dennis Eckart of Ohio quoted an article from the magazine *Chemical Week* complaining that the principal that polluters should pay was "crumbling." What's more, the magazine charged, the EPA was "undermining the program." Instead of aggressively pursuing polluters, the EPA was simply "footing the bill" with taxpayers' money.

Most of the criticism of the Superfund was not directed against the program itself, but at the way it was run. Fortuna, for example, argued that SARA, in particular, was well written. He charged, however, that there had been "active intervention" by the Superfund administrators to "undermine" those laws. Early charged the same administrators with "making cleanup decisions outside the law, failing to adequately protect public health and the environment, and creating loopholes for toxic waste dumpers." The Superfund program could be made to work, he argued, but not without "intensive oversight and constant prodding" by Congress.

Some committee members defended Superfund, at least in part. The ranking Republican on the House Committee, Representative Thomas Bliley of Ohio, ironically suggested that Superfund's critics may have been partly to blame for the agency's slowness. The fear that whatever decision they reached on cleaning up a site would be subject to harsh criticism, if not outright attack, may have made Superfund officials reluctant to come to any decision at all.

The only really spirited defense of Superfund administrators, however, came from the officials themselves. They argued that they had done the best they could in a difficult position. Their slowness had not come from any desire to drag things out, they insisted, but from a desire to come to the best possible decisions about which methods to use to clean up the different sites.

William Wallace, a hazardous waste management consultant, argued that the officials' desire may have been part of the problem. He argued, in essence, that there is no perfect cleanup method—no decision that cannot be criticized. Environmentalists and Superfund officials alike might be better off, he seemed to suggest, if everyone would stop trying to be so thorough and get on with the job of cleaning up the nation's hazardous waste sites.

Representative Bliley gave the Superfund program a mixed report card at best. Judged by meeting deadlines and by its undoubted ability to spend money, he said the program had been a success. However, judged by the Superfund's ability to fulfill its duty to protect human health and the environment, the program was not a success. There was, he concluded, "much room for improvement."

The acting chairman of the committee, Representative Dennis Eckart, agreed. "All is not well [with the Superfund], particularly in the face of remedial activity, the vigor of the enforcement program, and the selection of cleanup remedies." Nonetheless, he believed that "the Superfund statute is sound and workable, but it is not necessarily being properly administered or enforced."

The conclusion seems to be that the future effectiveness of Superfund will depend on the people in charge of it. If they are aggressive and determined, Superfund may be able to clean up the nation's most dangerous existing toxic waste sites—and to make the polluters pay for doing it. If they are not, as the administrators of the 1980s were not, many of the sites will remain as dangerous as ever.

CHAPTER NINE

HOPE FOR

THE FUTURE

IN this book, we have seen what a dangerous enemy toxic waste can be. Left unopposed, it can ravage the environment and destroy the public's health and safety. Yet until very recently, we have left ourselves almost undefended against it. We have allowed toxic wastes of all kinds to invade our environment—to clutter up our land, to poison our lakes, rivers, and oceans, and to pollute our air.

It is only in recent decades that we have come to see this invading enemy for the deadly menace that it is. Now, at last, we have begun to fight back. Many elements of our society have joined in the battle. Prompted by environmentalists, the public at large has come to see the danger. Prompted by the public, the government has moved to regulate industry. Prompted by the government, many private businesses are making greater efforts than ever before to limit the toxic wastes they generate and to dispose of them as safely as they can. At the same time, scientists and engineers have come up with new ways to treat and dispose of the toxic wastes that are generated. At last, Congress has committed the government to eliminate the danger of toxic wastes altogether.

There has been a growing awareness on the part of all these elements of society that the struggle against toxic wastes is more than a battle. It is a war: a war for survival.

It is time to ask how that war is going.

VICTORIES

Victories have been won on many fronts in the war against toxic wastes. According to Secretary of the Interior Donald Hodel, the United States has spent more money to clean up the environment than any other country on Earth. However controversial the EPA and its Superfund program have been, several toxic waste sites have been cleaned up. Additionally, hundreds of safe TSDs have been licensed and hundreds of unsafe TSDs have been shut down.

Some of the most striking victories have been won in the battle against water pollution. Once-filthy rivers, like the Delaware, have been cleaned up. Even more impressive has been the joint U.S.-Canadian effort to clean up the mighty Great Lakes.

Taken together, those five lakes comprising the Great Lakes form the largest body of fresh water in the world. Their vast surfaces cover an area of 95,000 square miles. Two decades ago, scientists believed the lakes were in danger of dying. Sewage from the cities along the lakeshores was fouling the waters. Industrial effluents from scores of paper mills and manufacturing plants were pouring daily doses of 400 different chemicals into the poisonous "stew." Fish and other sea life in the lakes were being strangled by pollution, and the lakes' multibillion dollar recreation industry was in danger of being strangled as well.

Thanks to a massive $9 billion effort by the United States and Canada, the amount of wastes being poured into the lakes has been slashed to a fraction of what it once was. As a result, this enormous fresh water resource is cleaner than it has been in decades.

There have been major victories in the battle against solid wastes and air pollution as well. Lead has been removed from house paints and from most of the gasoline sold for use in automobiles. Asbestos has been removed from thousands of school buildings. Pesticides such as dichlorodiphenyl tri-chloroethane, commonly known as DDT, and several other deadly chemicals can no longer be used in the United States.

Government pressure has made sure that emission control devices are put on all automobiles. The devices have greatly reduced the levels of hydrocarbons and carbon monoxide given off by individual automobiles. At the same time, government regulations have significantly cut down the amount of toxic smoke and particulates being poured out of the nation's smoke-stacks. By mid-1988, some 200 U.S. communities that had once dumped their municipal wastes into the oceans had stopped doing so.

DEFEATS

Yet as impressive as all these victories have been, they have not solved the problem of toxic wastes. The rate at which some kinds of wastes are being added to the environment has slowed down, but the total amount of toxic wastes in the environment has continued to increase.

On the land, the overwhelming majority of the hazardous waste sites in the United States remain as dangerous as they ever were. In the meantime, the nuclear power and defense indus-tries continue to pile up high-level nuclear wastes without any real plan for disposing of it.

Despite the fact that the Clean Water Act of 1972 ordered an end to the discharge of toxic wastes into lakes and rivers by 1985, poisonous effluents continue to pour into them. Even the impressive measures taken to clean up the Great Lakes have only partially succeeded. U.S. and Canadian health officials continue to warn that it is unsafe to eat many kinds of fish that are caught in the lakes. In 1988, health officials warned pregnant women not to eat any fish from Lake Michigan at all.

Meanwhile, many of our other lakes and rivers are unsafe either to fish or to swim in, much less to drink from. Summer after summer, scores of beaches are closed: some because of sewage, some because of industrial sludges, and some because of agricultural or urban runoff.

Even the vast oceans have been poisoned. Although many coastal cities have stopped dumping their sewage into them, many others have not—including some of the biggest. The EPA originally ordered cities to end all dumping in the Atlantic Ocean by December 31, 1981. Despite that order, dumping in that ocean reached its worst crisis so far in 1988, seven years *after* that deadline. Reluctantly, Congress moved in 1988 to change the deadline for ending dumping to 1992, eleven years after the original deadline. Even then—and despite the tons of wastes that were fouling the Atlantic's beaches that summer—several cities protested that they couldn't possibly stop dumping sewage in the ocean that soon. Among the protestors was New York City's mayor, Ed Koch. Asked by a frustrated congressman when New York *would* be ready to end its dumping, Koch said he just didn't know.

The air may be even more seriously polluted than the land and the water. In spite of all the controls on automobile and industrial emissions since 1965, the ozone levels measured in the summer of 1988 were the highest ever. Worst of all, the menacing trio of environmental time bombs—acid rain, the greenhouse effect, and the depletion of the ozone layer—are ticking away at a steadily faster rate.

The fact is, we are losing the war against toxic wastes. There is another, even more important fact as well. The war is not yet lost. Environmental experts agree that there is still time to win it—time to save the environment and ourselves. In the rest of this chapter we will discuss what will be necessary to do this.

AN INTERNATIONAL EFFORT

The war on toxic wastes is an unusual war. It is a war in which all the countries of the world have to be on the same side: the side of survival.

Yet it is hard for nations to cooperate in fighting this global war. Different countries have different economic needs. Toxic wastes are generated in efforts to fill those needs. A country with many energy resources might find it relatively easy to call for an end to the use of a polluting energy source like coal, for example. How, though, can another country, whose only energy resource is coal, be expected to go along? On the other hand, a small country with few paved roads might find it easy to agree to a limit on the number of cars. What about a huge country like the United States or Canada, which bases much of its way of life on the automobile? Yet coal burned anywhere in the world and gasoline burned anywhere in the world, affect the same atmosphere that supports us all.

In the mid-1980s, an international committee, the World Commission on Environment and Development, was set up to study this issue. The commission was chaired by Prime Minister Gro Brundtland of Norway. She and twenty-two experts from around the world studied and discussed the issue for two and one-half years. What is needed, according to the Brundtland Commission Report, which was issued in 1987, is a global program of sustainable development; that is, a policy of worldwide economic growth that takes into account the needs of all countries. Such a program must meet the needs of all the people alive today and meet the needs of our children—and their children and their children and their children's children. The commission concluded that this kind of sustainable development is more than possible. It is absolutely necessary. One of the vital elements of any program of sustainable development is the improved management of toxic wastes.

There have been some encouraging steps toward international cooperation in the management of toxic wastes in recent years. At a June 1988 economic summit meeting in Toronto, Canada, the leaders of the major western industrialized countries endorsed the concept of sustainable development. The World Bank, which makes loans for development projects in the Third World, has even begun to consider the need for sustainable development when deciding which loans to grant.

Even earlier, in 1987, diplomats from fifty nations had worked out a landmark agreement that may serve as a model for future international cooperation. Known as the "Montreal Protocol," it is aimed at saving the Earth's ozone layer. It requires the signing nations to freeze releases of halons and CFCs (chlorofluorocarbons) at 1986 levels and to cut the amount of CFCs released into the atmosphere in half by 1999. In the meantime, the countries agreed to cooperate in research on the ozone layer.

Recognizing the special needs of the economically underdeveloped countries, the protocol allows some exceptions. Underdeveloped countries will be able to double their production of CFCs for refrigeration purposes over the next ten years. By that time, scientists believe, they will have found new, nontoxic substitutes for the ozone-destroying chemicals.

Thirty-one countries signed the protocol immediately. Several others, including the Soviet Union, are expected to sign before the agreement goes into effect in 1989. Many of these same countries plan to meet again in 1992 to discuss progress on major environmental issues and to plan for future action.

In the meantime, thirty-five European nations have negotiated a similar agreement, designed to freeze their emissions of nitrogen oxides.

Environmental problems are an international concern. In Brazil, for example, acid rain has destroyed the leaves of these trees that once formed a dense forest surrounding the town of Cubatao. AP/Wide World Photos

CONSERVATION

The single most important thing that needs to be done to control toxic wastes is also the most obvious: We need to produce fewer of them. As the environmental researcher Walter Hang said: "As long as we continue to generate more and more waste, we're always going to have more and more problems."

The first step in reducing toxic wastes is to reduce the need for generating them in the first place. That means conservation. As we have seen, even many products that never become toxic wastes themselves can cause the generation of toxic wastes when they are made. Because of this, virtually any kind of conservation can be a weapon in the war against toxic wastes.

Some kinds of conservation can help in other ways as well. They include conservation of the vast forests that help to make life on Earth possible. These forests are a toxic waste management tool in themselves. As long as there are gasoline-powered cars, we will continue to pour carbon dioxide into the atmosphere. Preserving the forests is a major step in managing that threat to the environment.

From the tropical rain forests of Brazil to the timber stands of North America, the great forests are the lungs of our planet. they "breathe" much like we do, only in reverse. They take in carbon dioxide and give out oxygen. Most people are aware that the oxygen the forest gives out contributes to the atmosphere we breathe. Many people are unaware that the carbon dioxide they take in helps reduce the excess CO_2 that would otherwise intensify the greenhouse effect.

In the past few decades, the great forests have been disappearing at an alarming rate. According to Canada's Environment Minister Tom McMillan: "This year alone [1988], humanity will cut down 20 million hectares of forest—a landmass nearly equivalent to the size of the United Kingdom. In Ethiopia, for example, forest cover has shrunk from 30% of the total country only four years ago to a mere 1% today." This incredible destruction is eating away at the planet's ability to handle the increasing amount of carbon dioxide that we produce.

At the moment, very little is being done to replace the forests that are being lost. In the tropical regions of the world, only about one tenth of the trees that are cut down are replaced. According to McMillan, in some places it is only one in thirty. Even in an environmentally aware nation like Canada, only about one-fourth of the trees that are cut for timber are being replaced.

Stopping this widespread deforestation would help significantly to reduce the greenhouse effect. A massive, worldwide effort at *re*forestation would help even more.

ENERGY CONSERVATION

Conserving energy is at least as important as conserving the great forests. Lowering energy use cuts down on the use of the fossil fuels that contribute to many of the worst forms of air pollution. The less coal, petroleum products, and other fossil fuels we burn, the less carbon dioxide, sulphur dioxide, ozone, and VOCs will be added to the air.

There are several ways to cut down on energy use. Some are easy. One immediate possibility is to substitute fluorescent lights for incandescent bulbs wherever possible. It's been estimated that simply using fluorescent lighting in all public places would cut down total energy use in the United States by about 20 percent. Substituting buses and subways for cars in big cities would cut energy use —and toxic wastes in the air—much more.

Products that burn natural gas can be substituted for those that burn oil whenever possible. Gas-burning furnaces, for example, can be easily substituted for oil burners. Although natural gas is also a fossil fuel, it burns more efficiently than oil and sends less pollution into the air. The goal should be to stop using fossil fuels altogether by finding new and cleaner alternatives for them. Development of solar, wind, and other renewable energy sources would go far to lower the total amount of airborne toxic wastes.

Many Americans fear that conservation—and particularly a reduction in energy use—would cut into their standard of living. They believe that energy use and economic growth are inevitably tied together. After all, the Industrial Revolution, which led to modern economic development, was fueled by coal and petroleum. Many environmental experts disagree. As Mohamed El-Ashry of the World Resource Institute declares, "we can have our cake and eat it too."

El-Ashry, Donald Hodel, and others point to countries that maintain high standards of living while using much less energy than we do. Although they have living standards as high as ours, Japan and West Germany use only about half as much energy per person as in the United States.

Japan, in fact, has led the way in the conservation of both energy and raw materials. In the years since 1973, it has cut the amount of energy and raw materials that go into each unit of industrial production by 60 percent. During those same years, Japan's manufacturing industries have provided increasingly strong competition for the industries of the more wasteful West.

Even in the United States, economic growth and growing energy use have not always gone hand in hand. In recent years, they have actually moved in opposite directions. Between 1980 and 1985, for example, the U.S. gross national product (which measures production of goods and services) went from $2,732 billion to $4,010 billion. Over the same period, total personal income grew from $2,259 billion to $3,327 billion. Also during that time, energy consumption actually went down.

WHAT THE GOVERNMENT CAN DO

We have already discussed the government's present role in regulating toxic wastes. Many environmentalists, including Allen Hershkowitz of Municipal Recycling Associates and Michael Oppenheimer of the Environmental Defense Fund, believe that the federal government should expand its regulatory role.

There is virtually no effective federal regulation of medical wastes, for example. Widely differing state rules have led to offshore dumping and have encouraged interstate transportation of medical wastes in search of the most lenient state in which to dump them. Strictly enforced federal regulation of medical waste disposal would help to cut down on such practices.

The government's role, however, in toxic waste management could go beyond regulation, whether strict or otherwise. The environmentalist Cousteau Society, suggests that the United States (and other countries) should establish a "Department of the Future." Its job would be to prepare for the future by protecting the environment today.

Both state and federal governments can offer incentives to businesses and individuals who reduce energy use, help clean up the environment, and recycle, reuse, or convert their toxic wastes. In this area, the United States has many examples to learn from. Japan, Canada, West Germany, the Netherlands, and Denmark already offer tax benefits to companies that cut down waste production. Some countries also give financial help to companies in the form of grants and loans to encourage recycling.

Here in the United States, 29 states have some kind of program to cut down on wastes. These programs assist businesses and other institutions in cutting down their toxic wastes in a variety of ways. In recent years, the EPA has shown signs that it may come up with similar programs on the federal level.

American environmentalists believe that the federal government has a special role to play on the international scene as well. As one of the major generators of toxic wastes, the United States has an obligation to participate in—if not to lead—international efforts to solve toxic waste and other pollution problems.

Any final victory in the war on toxic wastes will certainly require action and cooperation on the national and international level. But this is not enough. As the Canadian environmentalist Rene Dubos said, nations and individuals alike need to "think globally, but act locally."

In the words of Tom McMillan, that

famous dictum...is even more relevant today than when he first said it a decade and a half ago. Sluggish progress on the international front is no excuse for inaction [by single nations], any more than lack of progress by national governments justifies complacency by individuals. Action is required at all levels.

WHAT BUSINESSES CAN DO

Among the institutions that must act if the war on toxic wastes is to be won are the private businesses that generate so much of our toxic wastes. The EPA has suggested a number of steps that almost any business can take to reduce the amount of toxic wastes it produces.

- As a first step, the business should investigate its current practices. It should examine every raw material and finished product it purchases and determine which have the potential of becoming toxic wastes. Wherever possible, it should substitute nontoxic materials for toxic ones.

- The business should train its employees in handling toxic materials, making sure that they do not generate more wastes than necessary through carelessness or poor training.

- All equipment used in the business should be as efficient as possible to cut down on waste of all kinds. When necessary, equipment should be changed or replaced to increase efficiency. Strict preventive maintenance programs should always be in place to keep all machinery running at top efficiency.

- All manufacturing processes should be designed to promote waste reduction at every step along the way. Different kinds of wastes should be separated from each other. Segregated wastes are easier to reuse, or to dispose of efficiently, than those that are mixed together. Whenever possible, wastes should be reused, recycled, or converted into usable materials.

- When a company cannot recycle or reuse its own wastes, it should try to find another company that can. If possible, it should exchange wastes with other companies, each using the wastes that the other cannot use.

WHAT INDIVIDUALS CAN DO

Ultimately, it is up to each of us—as citizens and as consumers— to fight the war against toxic wastes. We must learn to conserve our resources, to do our part to generate as little toxic waste as possible, and to dispose of our wastes as efficiently and safely as possible.

Much like businesses, individuals should buy and use nontoxic, rather than toxic, products whenever they can. This rarely requires sacrifice, just some thought. The following are just a few of many possible examples of good choices consumers can make.

- When choosing a hair spray, deodorant, or shaving cream, aerosol cans should be avoided. There is almost always an equally effective cream, roll-on, or nonaerosol spray available.

- When choosing cleaning products, avoid those containing caustic chemicals of any kind. Many oven or drain cleaners, for example, contain lye, sodium hydroxide, or potassium hydroxide, all of which eventually end up as toxic wastes. Nontoxic baking soda can be an effective substitute for a scouring agent, while boiling water or a metal plumbing "snake" will usually free a clogged drain.

- Be especially careful in choosing herbicides (weedkillers) and pesticides and any other kind of product containing poisons. When possible, try to get along without them.

- Even when choosing shoe polish, pick one that doesn't contain toxic chemicals such as trichloroethylene, methylene chloride, or nitrobenzene. Although almost all paints contain some toxic substances, water-based paints are best because they don't contain volatile hydrocarbons in the form of solvents.

- Whatever products a consumer chooses, he or she should read the labels carefully. In general, products should be used only in ways recommended on the label. Special attention should be given to any instruction that contains a word like "Caution," "Warning," or "Danger." These are clear signals that the product contains at least one toxic substance. At the same time, however, consumers should be aware that labels are not always accurate and are rarely complete. The fact that no apparently toxic ingredient is listed on the label, for example, is not proof that there is no toxic ingredient in the product.

- You can limit the toxic wastes you will eventually have to dispose of by buying only what they need to use. Any toxic products left unused usually should be stored in the container it came in. This cuts down the chance of accidents and avoids contaminating a second container. When possible, sharing toxic products with someone else is better than throwing them away or storing them indefinitely yourself.

- When disposing of products that contain toxic substances, be careful to follow any disposal instructions on the label. Some kinds of wastes have to be transported to a special disposal site. Waste oil from automobiles, for example, always should be taken to a waste oil depository. Many communities have some kind of special hazardous waste collection program available. Check with your local city hall to find out about yours.

There are several important "don'ts" when disposing of any toxic wastes:

- Don't attempt to burn products that contain toxic chemicals.

- Don't mix toxic substances together. Some chemicals are more dangerous when combined with others.

- Don't pour toxics out on the ground, or onto a street or pathway of any kind, whether paved or unpaved.

- Don't bury them.

- Don't pour them down the drain, flush them down the toilet, or dump them into the sewer system.

- Don't reuse a container that has been used to hold pesticides or any other toxic chemicals for any other purpose.

In addition to all the "don'ts," there is one very important "do": Do recycle all wastes possible, whether toxic or not. Most communities have sites where paper, aluminum cans, glass, and other recyclable products can be easily dropped off. Find out about these facilities in your community and use them.

AN IMPORTANT LAST WORD

If all of us—individuals, businesses, and governments—do our part, the war on toxic wastes can be won. We have the time we need to win it. But the clock is already ticking. When Prime Minister Brundtland was asked to sum up the historic Brundtland Commission Report as briefly as possible, she said she could do it in a single word: Her answer was the key to victory in the war against toxic wastes—"Now. We must act now."

BIBLIOGRAPHY

BOOKS

A Hazardous Waste Primer. Washington, D.C.: League of Women Voters Education Fund, 1980.

Block, Alan A., and Scarpitti, Frank R. *Poisoning for Profit*. New York: William Morrow and Company, 1985.

Brown, Michael. *Laying Waste: The Poisoning of America by Toxic Chemicals*. New York: Pantheon, 1980.

Epstein, Samuel S.; Brown, Lester O.; and Pope, Carl. *Hazardous Waste in America*. San Francisco: Sierra Club Books, 1982.

Household Pollutants Guide. Center for Science in the Public Interest. Garden City, N.Y.: Anchor Press/Doubleday, 1978.

Moran, Joseph M.; Morgan, Michael D.; and Wiersma, James H. *Introduction to Environmental Science*. San Francisco: W.H. Freeman and Company, 1980.

ARTICLES

Friend, Tim. "Medical Waste Crisis Grips USA." *USA Today*, August 9, 1988, p. 1.

Morganthau, Tom, et al. "Don't Go Near the Water." *Newsweek*, August 1, 1988, p. 42.

Shabecoff, Philip. "Ozone Pollution Is Found at Peak in Summer Heat." *New York Times*, July 31, 1988, p. 1.

"Superfund: Looking Back, Looking Ahead." *EPA Journal*, Special Section, January-February 1987, pp. 13-35.

Wingerson, Lois. "No More Toxic Wastes." *New Scientist*, June 18, 1987, pp. 54-58.

OTHER PUBLICATIONS

Air Matters. Wisconsin Department of Natural Resources Bureau of Air Management vol. 2, no. 1, Spring 1984.

Alternatives to Household Hazardous Waste. Citizens for a Better Environment Fact Sheet. Undated.

Buggie, Frederick D., and Gurman, Richard. *Toward Effective and Equitable Pollution Control Regulation*. New York: American Management Association, 1972.

"Hazardous Waste Management." Pamphlet. Washington, D.C.: American Chemical Society, 1984.

Hazardous Waste Management: Recent Changes and Policy Alternatives. Washington, D.C.: U.S. Congressional Budget Office, 1985.

Henry, Harold W. *Pollution Control: Corporate Responses*. New York: American Management Association, 1974.

Lee, Martin R. *Toxic Waste Incineration at Sea*. CRS Issue Brief. Washington, D.C.: Congressional Research Service, 1987.

McCarthy, James E. *Hazardous Waste Management: RCRA Oversight in the 100th Congress*. CRS Issue Brief. Washington, D.C.: Congressional Research Service, 1988.

McMillan, Tom. "Notes for Remarks by the Honorable Tom McMillan, Lawrence River," June 3, 1988.

McMillan, Tom. Speech to the Sierra Club, May 7, 1988.

Reisch, Mark E. Anthony. *The Superfund Amendments and Reauthorization Act of 1986.* CRS Issue Brief. Washington, D.C.: Congressional Research Service, 1988.

Serious Reduction of Hazardous Waste for Pollution Prevention and Industrial Efficiency. Washington, D.C.: U.S. Congress Office of Technology Assessment, 1986.

Solid Wastes. Environmental Science and Technology Reprint. Washington, D.C.: American Chemical Society.

Superfund Strategy. Washington, D.C.: U.S. Congress Office of Technology Assessment, 1985.

Technologies and Management Strategies for Hazardous Waste Control. Washington, D.C.: U.S. Congress Office of Technology Assessment, 1983.

Waste Minimization—Environmental Quality with Economic Benefits. Washington, D.C.: U.S. EPA Office of Solid Waste and Emergency Response, 1987.

INDEX

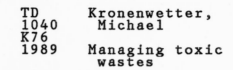